MORE PARKHURST TALES

OTHER BOOKS BY NORMAN PARKER FOR
SMITH GRYPHON

Parkhurst Tales: A Murderer's Life in Britain's Toughest Jail
The Goldfish Bowl: Inside the Hard and Secret World of a Lifer

MORE PARKHURST TALES

SENSATIONAL REAL-LIFE
STORIES BY A MURDERER INSIDE
BRITAIN'S MOST NOTORIOUS JAIL

NORMAN PARKER

SMITH GRYPHON
PUBLISHERS

First published in Great Britain in 1997 by
SMITH GRYPHON LIMITED
12 Bridge Wharf
156 Caledonian Road
London N1 9UU

A CIP catalogue record for this book is available from the British Library

ISBN 1 85685 134 6

Typeset by Action Typsetting Limited, Gloucester
Printed and bound in Great Britain by Butler & Tanner Ltd, Frome

Contents

Glossary   vii

Preface: To Hollywood   1

Introduction: On Making 'Bad' Men Worse   3

1   Give 'Em a Body   5

2   The Centre   19

3   The Treatment Queue   31

4   Wally and the Turds   34

5   The Nine Lives of 'Top-cat'   44

6   The Mackerel   64

7   Baron Blunt   70

8   Nut-Nut   82

9   Mr Nice-guy   87

10 The Poof Doctor   93

11 Somebody Loves a Fairy at 40   98

12 Hitler's Child   115

13 The Albany Wall Game   146

14 Of Escapes, Principles and Prison Politics   192

For the ultimate 'chap',
honourable, loyal, courageous,
my mum

Glossary

AG   Assistant Governor

'A' list   the highest security category of prisoner

Albany   top-security jail on the Isle of Wight

bang-up   lock up

bird   prison sentence, time

bit of work   a criminal venture, i.e. a robbery

blade   home-made knife

block   punishment block (*see also* chokey)

book   horse-racing book

bridge   in a prison, a short landing running across the wing, joining the two long landings on either side

Broadmoor   top-security hospital for the criminally insane, in Berkshire

Chaps   an almost mythical grouping of criminals whose ethos includes: professionalism in the pursuit of crime; loyalty to others of their kind; hatred of and non-cooperation with authority; and courage. Many aspire to membership, few qualify

chief   chief officer, the most senior uniformed officer in the jail

chokey   punishment block

civvy   civilian instructor

'E' man   someone on the 'escape list', placed there for having escaped, attempting to escape or being suspected of planning to escape

face   notorious or influential criminal with some standing within the criminal fraternity – 'to be a face'

food-boat   arrangement where several prisoners chip in to cover the expense of a shared meal

fours and fives   in prison, the fourth and fifth landings

Gartree   top-security, category–A prison near Market Harborough, Leicestershire

gavolt rumpus

GBH grievous bodily harm

grass to inform, an informer

heavy mob (the) the riot squad

hooch home-brewed booze

Jack the Hat Jack McVitie, murdered by Ron and Reg Kray

joey small parcel, usually of contraband

khazi toilet

Long Lartin Category–A top-security prison near Evesham, Worcestershire

make one to join in some illegal venture – e.g. an escape

Maze (the) top-security prison near Lisburn, County Antrim, Northern Ireland (a.k.a. Long Kesh)

Moor (the) Dartmoor Prison in Devon

nitto look out! beware!

nonce sex offender

off, to be for trouble to break out

ones in a prison, the lowest landing

Old Bill the police

on the book if you are an 'A' or 'E' man, a small book with your photo in it goes everywhere you go

Parkhurst one of two maximum-security prisons on the Isle of Wight, the other being Albany

patches distinctive clothing worn by man on the 'escape list' (*see* 'E' man). The trousers have bright yellow stripes down the outside seams, and there are bright yellow patches on jacket and trouser pockets

PO principal officer

POA Prison Officers' Association, their union

pony crap, shit

pop escape attempt

Rampton top-security hospital for the criminally insane, in Nottinghamshire

raver homosexual, poof

ready-eye   planned trap set by the police

rec   'recommendation', minimum term to be served

ringer   stolen car or double (twin)

Rule 43   indefinite segregation, either for self-protection or because 'Good Order, and Discipline' may be violated (i.e. the prisoner is deemed subversive)

screw   prison warder

Scrubs (the)   Wormwood Scrubs prison in West London

shanghaied   transferred immediately to another prison

snout   tobacco

SO   senior officer

spiel   gambling club, often illegal

spin   search

stage rooms   association rooms, where prisoners have their recreation periods

straightened   corrupted

tea-boat   arrangement whereby several prisoners chip in to cover the expense of sharing a pot of tea

The Twins   Ron and Reg Kray

threes   in a prison, the third landing

tie-up   a robbery, usually in a private house, during which people are tied up

tool   weapon

two stretch   two-year sentence

twos   in a prison, the second landing

VC   Visiting Committee: magistrates who adjudicate on serious prison offences

volley   to accuse verbally

white shirt   senior officer, either POA or a SO

Preface: To Hollywood

Dear Hollywood

Thank you for the murderous images that filled and fuelled my younger years. Thank you for Bronson, Schwarzenegger, Stallone and all the other violent killers who rampaged across the screen. At times I became quite confused. Could murder and mayhem be so wrong when all my favourite heroes were doing it?

Mickey and Mallory were really cool; Natural Born Heroes, they killed by the score.

Thank you especially for Hannibal Lector. Urbane, charming, witty, interesting, what a shame he killed and ate people on the side. How was I to know that this glamorized, sanitized portrayal was not the true nature of the serial killer?

For decades I travelled through the bowels of our prison system, searching for the heroes of my youth. You can imagine my disappointment when the man never once bore much resemblance to the myth. The serial killers were all sick, disgusting people; the rapists singularly unattractive; the gangsters often selfish and mean-spirited. You have misled a whole generation.

But perhaps my journey hasn't been completely in vain. From my experience, let me now show you the true nature of the beast. Come into my world for a while and marvel at the abominations in human form. Bad, most certainly. But also quite mad. Sad even. Glamorous and attractive? Not ever.

Hollywood, how could you have got it so wrong?

NORMAN PARKER, 1996

Introduction: On Making 'Bad' Men Worse

THIS BOOK, IN addition to the stories set in Parkhurst, includes incidents from Wakefield, Wandsworth, Albany, Long Lartin and Wormwood Scrubs prisons. Strictly speaking, I have employed a degree of artistic licence in using the title *More Parkhurst Tales*. However, Parkhurst is probably our most notorious and widely known prison, and I use it as an icon for all our long-term jails.

All the stories are true. However, I have sometimes changed names, dates and small details of description to avoid embarrassing men who have long since left prison behind them. Further, as the prison authorities create and control all official records, it is not perhaps surprising that their account of events might differ from mine. Our libel laws being what they are, a jury might well believe the official version rather than that given by ex-cons. Therefore, in places I have been deliberately vague.

I most sincerely believe that what I do in describing life in our prisons is important in that it informs the debate. Crime and the Criminal Justice System is one of the most contentious issues of our time. Everybody seems to have an opinion about it. Unfortunately, the vast majority of this opinion is, in my view, singularly ill-informed.

Our prison system is secretive, wasteful, poorly managed and badly run. It can only make 'bad' men and women worse. It is therefore dysfunctional to society as a whole. It is my intention to bring this to the notice of the general public through my writing. Those who choose not to believe me can always listen to the Home Secretary.

1. Give 'Em a Body

ROBERT JOHN WEXLER had never read Machiavelli, yet he would have intuitively understood the basic ethos of the creed. Not on any intellectual level, of course – Robert Wexler wasn't in the least cerebral. However, at a gut level, amongst his primal urges, it would have made very good sense indeed.

Of course a Prince should be feared rather than loved. It had become Robert's main aim in life. To be feared by as many people as possible. Because love had never done anything for him, not even to get him noticed, however fleetingly.

His first murder had been largely frustration. And LSD. He could barely remember now the haze that seemed to surround him through that period. He had been just 20 and a Scouse lad in London. If he had thought that the South would be more understanding of his homosexuality than his native North, then he was soon disappointed. London in the mid-Seventies was almost as homophobic as the rest of the country. His kind were still poofs and queers to most people. With that point of view came the scorn and derision. And the emphasis that a queer wasn't a proper man, that he lacked manly qualities.

Robert was already desperately unsure of himself. He realized that his strange looks and tall skinny frame endeared him to few. The secret guilt over his sexuality was the catalyst that triggered the seething rage.

It was ironic that the victim was the one person who had noticed him and shown him some affection. Barry had allowed him to stay at his rundown council flat. They regularly tripped together. They also became lovers. During one trip, Barry had become the personification of the illicit passion that caused Robert so much guilt.

The actual killing had been almost surreal, like some kind of acid flashback. He had observed himself as he plunged the knife again and again into Barry's flesh. The screams seemed so frantic; the blood so vivid.

There had never been any real plan, so Robert hadn't prepared his escape. He was soon caught. The trial at the Old Bailey surprised him in only one respect. He had always known that he viewed the world in a strange way. Surely others didn't feel such pain and despair as a matter of course? But he had never considered himself to be mad. And as much as he tried to disguise the implications, to be found guilty of manslaughter not murder, because of diminished responsibility, meant that he was officially insane.

The 'hospital order' had sent him to Broadmoor 'without limit of time'. In short, a life sentence in a top-security hospital for the criminally insane. Depressingly, here he found others of his ilk. Men and women obsessed with a particular world-vision; one that occupied all their waking moments and stressed them to the point of purgatory.

If Robert had thought that the killing would afford him some new kind of status, would set him over and above the next person, he didn't find it so in Broadmoor. There were hundreds of patients in that hospital who had killed, often more prolifically and in more brutal circumstances than Robert. Whereas before he had been just another faceless misfit in the big city, now he was just another faceless patient in a vast human warehouse.

But Robert had noticed something, had learned something, in the process of the killing. He had long been aware of the dark force that lurked at the fringes of his consciousness, birthed in frustration, nurtured by rage. At times it seemed very similar to rage. It was certainly utterly destructive and almost uncontrollable. He had learned to release it a little at a time. Sometimes its power frightened him. Although it seemed to be of him, he also felt it to be outside him. Part of some greater, infinitely more powerful, force.

But it served its purpose admirably. It drove him and gave him a courage that, although innately self-destructive, enabled him to pursue his vision. That vision wouldn't be realized at Broadmoor though. He had to move on. But how? He was a certified lunatic; it would be many years, if ever, before he could expect to be transferred.

However, he learned from some of the older patients, men who had been there for many years, that you could 'give 'em a body'. It was something half-way between a rumour and an old story, but received wisdom had it that if you killed someone in Broadmoor and were convicted of murder in an outside court, then you would be sent to do the rest of your sentence in a prison.

It didn't make sense really. For a man, already mad, deliberately to kill another man inside a lunatic asylum must surely be an act of madness. But one old patient told him that it was more an administrative measure than a legal one. The staff at Broadmoor considered that a strict and punitive prison regime would be better able to cope with someone so highly dangerous. It was quite a convenient solution for them.

Robert's first attempt proved an abysmal failure. There were no sharp or heavy weapons at Broadmoor. A victim had to be overpowered and throttled, a difficult task for someone who was hardly a warrior. He thought he had chosen someone weaker than himself. He had gone out of his way to befriend him first, so the attack would be unsuspected. But a strength born of desperation enabled the victim to fight him off.

Robert had spent some time in seclusion. The attack was noted in his hospital record, but he was never charged in an outside court. He resolved to make certain the next time.

However bizarre the personality, it wasn't difficult to find a kindred spirit in Broadmoor. Tom, also in his early 20s and from Liverpool, had killed a drinking partner. The killing was just as senseless and sordid as Robert's. He also shared his drug-raddled physique and nerdy looks.

One way in which Tom did differ, though, was that he had more carefully thought out his personal *Weltanschauung*. Not that it was deeply philosophical. However, it did have a certain order. Tom prayed to the Devil. He had struggled with the black-magic books he had read; he was no scholar. But it struck a chord in him. Not only did it excuse the cruel and selfish things he did, it positively encouraged them.

Robert wasn't at all interested in praying to anyone. He was the deity at the centre of his particular cosmos. However, if black magic was what it took to motivate Tom to join him in the venture, then so be it.

They were generally agreed that they would carry out the killing in the most outrageous and bizarre way possible. They were limited by both the weapons available and a suitable opportunity. They also had to decide on a victim.

Jimmy had already been at Broadmoor for several years. Still in his 20s, he had been sentenced for a string of arson attacks. He was no stranger to mental hospitals, having spent much of his youth in them. But he still had a chirpy good humour, even if he was quite argumentative. He had thought nothing of it when he had argued with a gay friend of Robert's. In the latter's mind, though, it was enough to seal his fate. Tom put it differently: 'The Devil has chosen him,' he avowed.

Finding the opportunity proved more difficult than finding the weapon. Tom had taken his radio to pieces. Part of the frame was a long, flat piece of metal. He spent several nights sharpening it on the stone window-sill. Soon he had a small, razor-sharp knife, which he concealed in the radio.

Robert had been secretly watching Jimmy's movements. In truth there was very little to observe. He went to the day room, the ward, the recess, all places that were in clear view of the nurses. Ideally, Robert would have liked some time, undisturbed, with his victim.

Suddenly it dawned on him. Just along one of the corridors, there was a small room that served as a shoe and boot store. Footwear that wasn't worn on the wards was stored here. Actually, it was little more than a deep cupboard, each side lined with footwear stacked on racks. The clue was the racking. Robert reasoned that if they could get their victim into the store-room, they could pull the racking out from the wall, so blocking the door. And by the time the nurses could break their way in, Jimmy would be long since dead.

The plan proved very simple to put into practice. They just waited for Jimmy to collect his shoes to go out on exercise. As he bent over in the store, tying his laces, they burst in.

Robert pulled the racking in front of the door as Tom grappled with Jimmy. Then he joined in. Jimmy was only small and was quickly overpowered. They bound him with pieces of torn sheet. Now they could take their time.

The nurses had run to the store when they heard the struggle. The door wouldn't budge, and the spy-hole had been blocked from the inside. As soon as they determined that it wasn't a nurse being held hostage, some of the urgency went out of the situation. Negotiations began.

To the seasoned negotiator it was already an unusual hostage-taking. They didn't seem to be asking for much. Just to be left alone really, with the threat that they would kill the hostage if the nurses tried to force their way in.

Secure in the store, Robert and Tom began to enjoy themselves. Although tense, both felt exhilarated as they revelled in the power of holding another's life in their hands. They had discussed in detail exactly what they were going to do. And if they could achieve their plan, they were sure it would gain them the fear and respect they so desired from the criminal fraternity.

Jimmy, helpless and whimpering in fear, was easily intimidated. First they impressed on him that he was going to be tortured and killed. Then they forced grovelling apologies for the slight on Robert's gay friend. As penance they forced him to perform fellatio on them both. Then they slowly garrotted Jimmy to death.

But they weren't finished yet. They had pondered long and hard on what final, unspeakable act they could carry out. One that would grab people's attention and fill them with dread.

'We should eat a piece of his brain,' Tom had suggested.

Now, with Jimmy dead at their feet, he got out his home-made knife.

The subsequent trial at the nearby Crown Court attracted little media attention. The reporters were remarkably restrained. Perhaps it was because the accused were mental patients. You could hardly castigate the insane and moralize to them. To some, the hospital was as much at fault as the culprits: 'It was a scandal that they had allowed such a thing to happen.' But there would be no inquiry. The judge listened to the evidence of the torture and murder, then sentenced them both to life imprisonment.

Robert Wexler was sent to Wakefield Prison. His arrival caused absolutely no stir whatsoever; Wakefield wasn't known locally as the 'House of Horrors' for nothing. There were hundreds of violent and dangerous killers, many of whom had been in the mental hospitals.

As for the enhanced respect and deference he had expected from those professional criminals he so looked up to, the hard men from London and Liverpool still regarded him as a freakish fool. They wouldn't have hesitated to attack him violently had he shown them any lack of respect. And as he was hardly warrior material, Robert could do little to change the situation.

Robert now realized that he had made a big mistake. It had all been for nothing. His life had changed, but very much for the worse. The harsh and punitive regime at Wakefield didn't compare to the well-resourced, therapeutic regime at Broadmoor. He thought about how he could get back there.

He still had his vision. There was no limit to the number of people he could kill, given a suitably weak victim and the right opportunity. He resolved to kill again. He felt confident, eager even. The ragelike feeling that Tom had called evil was strong in him. It drove him with an almost irresistible force now.

Within a few weeks of arriving at Wakefield, Robert was able to discern who were the most dominant and influential cons. Mostly they were from Liverpool and London. It was the latter who fascinated him though. More sophisticated than their Northern counterparts, they were both professional in their manner and extremely violent, though outwardly quite pleasant at times. How Robert longed to be like them.

But theirs was a closed society. Unless you were from London or known and respected by them, they wouldn't even talk to you. They regarded Robert as just another dangerous nutter, when they regarded him at all. They didn't fear him in the slightest. He was nothing 'one to one', and they moved in tight groups anyway.

Robert focused on one particular group which lived on his own wing. There were four of them: two bank robbers, a gangland killer and, unusually, a Scouse robber. They went everywhere together, as much for personal safety as for the enjoyment of each other's company in a strange jail so far from home.

Robert had managed to get on talking terms with one of the London robbers called Sam, who worked in the iron foundry and got through clean clothes at an alarming rate. Robert worked in the tailor's shop and had altered jeans and shirts for Sam, refusing to charge for the favour. This impressed Sam somewhat, because it was supposedly part of the code that 'your own' never charged each other for a favour. It was also quite convenient.

Robert waited his time. After about a month, during which he had altered several sets of clothes for Sam, he asked to speak to him in private. Sam had always known there was a good chance that Robert would ask a favour in return. But he was sufficiently influential and well off to grant most things. The request, though, surprised him. Robert wanted a knife!

Weapons were often made clandestinely in the foundry where Sam worked. However, it was a very serious matter indeed. Merely to be caught with a weapon could result in solitary confinement, loss of remission and, sometimes, an immediate transfer to a local prison. And if the weapon were subsequently used in a murder or other serious assault, the maker could be done as an accessory. Consequently, weapons were only made for close friends; always as a matter of duty and rarely charged for.

Robert was way out of line. As Sam gathered himself to volley him, the latter blurted out a reason that gave Sam pause.

'I want to kill a screw with it, Sam. I want to do a screw.'

Everyone hated the screws at Wakefield. It was a brutal, uncaring regime, and the screws enforced the rules enthusiastically. Many were ex-squaddies who had served in Northern Ireland and had become inured to suffering. Needless to say some hated Republican prisoners. This was only one aspect of their bigotry and prejudice though. They also hated Londoners and blacks with a passion. Some carried a National Front stickpin concealed behind their lapel, occasionally flashing it at the blacks they harassed.

Sam had a particular reason to hate screws. He had been beaten up by them in a London prison. Not these Wakefield screws admittedly. But as most screws regarded all cons as being just the same, so were they regarded in return.

A thoughtful gleam appeared in Sam's eye. 'If you say one word of this to anyone mate, even my pals, me and you'll really fall out,' he said.

'I know better than to say anything,' conceded Robert.

Sam took a couple of weeks to make the knife. Not that the actual job took that long. But in view of the use to which it would be put, Sam wanted to make sure that no one saw him do it.

Robert was standing in his cell one tea-time when Sam hurried in. Quickly, he thrust a rag-wrapped bundle into his hands and hurried out.

That evening, after lock-up, Robert examined it. The greasy rag revealed a long, flat piece of steel with razor-sharp edges that tapered to a point. He bound a strip of cloth around the blunt end to make a handle that was easy to grip. He now had a fearsome weapon.

He wasn't satisfied though. Fearing that Sam would never make the knife for him, Robert had bought a piece of hacksaw blade from an acquaintance. Now he used it to cut deep notches into the blade. It would still go in easily enough, but when it was pulled out the jagged edges would catch on flesh and sinew.

Robert hadn't given much thought to which screw he would kill. The prospect was a daunting one. The screws sometimes beat you half to death merely for punching one of them. They made it quite clear that they hardly cared what the cons did to each other, but if a screw were touched, you were really for it.

Robert had serious second thoughts. His long suit was madness and wickedness, not courage. He came up with a second plan. He would kill as many people as he was able, before the screws could stop him.

He went back to Sam. 'I've decided not to kill a screw,' he told him. 'It'd cause too much trouble. They'd close the nick down and take away all the privileges.' There was a strong element of truth in this, and Sam nodded in agreement. 'I'm gonna kill as many nonces and grasses as I can. So if you want to give me a couple of names, I'll do them for you.'

Sam was perfectly capable of dealing with his own enemies, however, he hated nonces and grasses almost as much as he hated the screws. 'Just make sure it IS nonces and grasses,' he growled.

It was Friday afternoon in the tailor's shop. Robert sat idle at his sewing machine, he had done his quota for the week. Before him, cut paper shapes lay on his work-surface. Carefully he folded them, so intent on the task he didn't see his neighbour looking over. As he finished he sat back. A production line of small paper coffins, each with a cross on the lid, lay in front of him.

Saturday was a day of rest for most cons. They played games, watched TV, cleaned their cells and went on exercise. All the cell doors were unlocked. The cons moved about freely as the screws congregated at the ends of the landings.

Robert was well aware that it was Saturday, but he didn't have recreation on his mind. Tucking the knife carefully inside his jeans, he started out on his mission.

It was just after breakfast, and the wing was quiet. Men still sat in their cells eating their meal. Robert made his way to the landing below and the cell of his mate, Shawn. Well, he wasn't actually a mate, Robert would argue with himself. They were in a tea-boat together. They also occasionally had sex. But he wasn't a friend. Definitely not a friend. Apart from anything else, Shawn was a nonce. In for molesting kids. This hadn't stopped Robert from taking tea and sex with him, but as far as Robert was concerned the category of 'nonce' superseded that of 'friend'.

Shawn was short, fat, fortyish and balding. He hadn't been up long, so he was still sleepy. Even if he had been wide awake, he wouldn't have suspected anything. He certainly regarded Robert as a friend.

As Shawn turned to prepare tea, Robert quickly pulled out the knife and plunged it into his neck. Grabbing the quivering head with one hand, he sawed away with the knife. In seconds it was over. Robert lowered the still gurgling form to the floor. Putting the knife down, he knelt to push the body under the bed. He arranged the counterpane so it hung to the floor.

Robert could relax now. Almost leisurely, he cleaned the gory blade with tissues. Carefully he concealed the knife down the front of his jeans again. He left the cell, banging the door behind him. He went looking for his next victim.

The prison-wise well know the value of a sixth sense, an ability to interpret nuances of meaning, understated tensions and performances slightly out of sync from the norm. It is survival specific for the dangerous long-term jails and mental hospitals. This talent is learned with great difficulty. A failure to do so can cost the unwary their life.

Wakefield was a dangerous jail. Security was designed to prevent escapes rather than stop violence amongst the cons. There was hardly a day without a serious, violent incident.

Perhaps the mark of the beast was plain on Robert that morning. Maybe the dilation of the eyes, the flare of the nostrils gave it away. For the next two hours Robert patrolled the landings trying to lure victims off to a private place. The inducements were a cup of coffee, a game of cards, the loan of magazines. All offers were politely, nervously rebuffed. Because there was something strange about Robert Wexler this morning. People couldn't put their collective fingers on it, but there was definitely something.

It was nearly noon, and dinner-time was approaching. The wings would be locked up for two hours, but first a count would be made. Shawn wouldn't be visible in his cell. A search would be made and the body found. Investigations would inevitably lead to Robert or, at the very least, he would have to ditch the knife.

But one victim wasn't enough. If he were really to make a name for himself there would have to be more. Frantically, he searched for another victim.

Will had killed his wife, but it was the only criminal act in an otherwise blameless life. Now in his late 40s, he had worked all his life and had two grown-up children. They didn't even write, silent condemnation for killing their mother. They just didn't understand it. He didn't understand it himself. The murder replayed in his mind like a badly remembered dream. Or, rather, nightmare. His life was a waking nightmare now. He was surrounded by all kinds of disturbed and violent people. He had always been a mild man himself.

He knew Robert from the tailor's shop. He was a strange lad in many ways, but their friendship only extended to sharing a tea-boat. He hardly ever saw him on the wing. He was surprised to see him now, standing in the doorway of his cell with magazines in his hand.

Robert accepted the invitation to come in, having anticipated it. Will was so polite and easygoing. It was hardly a challenge. But another victim was another victim.

As before, Robert jumped him from behind and sawed through his throat. It might have been Robert's imagination, but from the first thrust it seemed like Will didn't even struggle. Perhaps he had given up on life after he killed his wife.

There was no attempt at concealment now. Dinner-time bang-up was almost upon them, and the bodies would be found. It was time to declare his achievement. He would enjoy the look of surprise on the screws' faces.

PO Wells sat in the wing office on the 'ones'. It had been a busy morning. What with kit change, work parties, exercise and scores of applications he was ready for the quiet of the dinner-time break. He looked up as Robert Wexler came in. Secretly he cringed. He wondered what madness he would have to deal with now. Wexler was no problem on the wing, in fact you hardly knew he was there. But he was obviously quite mad. The PO wondered how he had ever got out of Broadmoor.

'What do you want, Wexler?' enquired the PO in a tone that emphasized he had had enough for the morning.

'You're two short up on the landing, boss,' came the mumbled, almost wheedling answer.

The PO looked at Wexler more closely. What was the idiot on about?

'What are you saying?' he demanded.

As he spoke, Wexler removed something from the top of his jeans and threw it down on the desk in front of him. 'I said you're two short up on the landing, boss.'

The message was clear, but the meaning wasn't. The PO looked down at the desk. His eyes bulged in astonishment and horror. The long dagger glinted cruelly in the bright office light. He could see the pieces of flesh and gore trapped in the grooves.

'Mr Wallace, Mr Wallace,' he cried, jumping to his feet. An intercommunicating door flew open, and his SO ran in. 'Get this man down the block,' he screamed, pointing at Wexler.

Together they walked slowly towards him, ushering him out of the office. 'Come here,' he screamed at a passing officer. 'Help Mr Wallace escort Wexler to the block immediately.'

The last victim was found first. The PO blanched as the officer announced his discovery. He blanched further when the second body was found. The rest of his day would be spent writing reports and making phone calls.

Sitting in the corner of a cell in the punishment block, Robert hardly felt any different. Admittedly, the zing of adrenalin still coursed his veins, but he knew that was merely transitory. He was just a man sitting alone in a cell. A man who had killed four people now, but in many ways quite an ordinary man nevertheless. Bare walls had no way of showing homage. This time, though, he was sure it would come.

And come it did, but hardly in the way that Robert

expected. Over in the hospital they built a special cell, a cell within a cell. There was the outer door, but once inside there was a six-foot space, then bars from floor to ceiling. Behind them was the cell proper. It was like a lion's cage at the zoo, but the lion was to be Robert. He was never to leave it, except to bathe or exercise. On those few occasions when he was unlocked, he would be accompanied by four screws at all times.

The trial was an anticlimax. His guilty plea was a formality. Once again the press was remarkably restrained. The proceedings barely made the national dailies, and the *Yorkshire Post* carried only a small piece. In sentencing him to life, though, the judge stressed the dangerousness of the defendant. And that was it.

Alone in his cage in Wakefield prison hospital, Robert pondered his fate. He was to be kept in this cell indefinitely. He would never mix with another prisoner. So where was the enhanced status he could now expect from his peers? Where the deference, the respect from other hard and dangerous men? Without an audience, there could hardly be a performance. In the absence of others, there was no such thing as self. He felt his personality begin to crumble. His life was purgatory now.

In lucid moments he mused on the nature of the force that had motivated him, that had driven him. He would call it by the name that Tom had given it now. In his ignorance, his naivety, he had thought he could control the evil. Could mould it to his purpose and achieve his destiny. It had only shown enough of itself to lure him onwards, but its goal was very clear now. Evil was the antithesis of all life. Robert Wexler was a life force. Its intention had been to destroy him all along.

Robert Wexler spent three years in his 'cage', before a television documentary about him forced a change. He was moved to top-security conditions, where he would be kept constantly under close supervision. He remains there today.

2. The Centre

OF ALL THE prisons in the country, Wandsworth was far and away the most feared and respected amongst the cons. Other jails might have had their moments – certain incidents or periods when a particularly brutal heavy mob had reigned – but 'Wanno' was in a class of its own.

Home Secretaries might come and go, liberal policies might be enacted, but Wandsworth was immovable and immutable. It was the flagship of the prison service. At least in the eyes of the screws if not the Home Office.

Wandsworth was a tight ship. There was no such thing as prisoner power, and as long as most of the screws there drew breath there never would be. It was a hotbed of militants. Their POA was one of the strongest in the country. If there were to be some sort of industrial action, you could safely bet that Wandsworth would be to the forefront.

Wandsworth was a local prison, a remand prison, a top-security prison and an allocation centre all rolled into one. On any given day, you could have as many as 1800 cons banged up. And banged up they would be, for there was little work and less association.

It was often said that you got exactly what you were entitled to at Wandsworth and not a jot more. That was true to a certain extent, but it was the absolute minimum you were entitled to.

The jail served London and the South, but there were cons from all over. Sentences ranged from 18 months right up to natural life. The toughest of the tough regularly walked through its gates. The screws managed to contain them though. Whoever it was, everyone toed the line. This was achieved by a very simple method: brutality. If you got out of your pram at Wandsworth, you could get very severely bashed up.

At the first sign of any trouble the alarm bell would sound. Every available screw would run to its source. This could mean 30 or 40 men, and many of the screws at Wandsworth were big lumps. With no hesitation whatsoever they would steam right in. Never mind who started it, or what the rights and the wrongs of the situation were, they would grab whosoever was at the centre of the mêlée and drag them away.

They would be carried bodily across the Centre and down on to E1. This was the punishment landing. Here they would be beaten, rammed head first into walls, their clothes torn from their bodies and, finally, thrown naked into a strip cell until the following morning.

On the subsequent Governor's Adjudication, or VC, the screws would all close ranks and lie in unison. To justify the beating, the con would be charged with assaulting a screw. He would inevitably be found guilty and lose six months' remission. You just couldn't win at Wandsworth.

In layout it was typical of all the old Victorian prisons. Five long galleried wings, A to E, radiated off a central hub. There were three separate wings, G, H and K, but these were used mostly for the nonces.

The Centre, the hub where the five wings conjoined was a circular area about 80 feet in diameter. Around the edge was a tiled pathway some 15 feet wide. Right in the middle was a gigantic metal grating, all of 50 feet across.

It was an amazing construction. Made out of cast metal, it comprised several sections. The actual grating was of a strange and intricate pattern. The darkness below was as impenetrable as that of the pit. No one knew what lay beneath.

In itself, in any other half-ways sane place, this would just have been an unusual architectural feature. In the hallowed halls of Wandsworth, though, the grating had come to assume an almost mystical significance. Its whole surface had been polished until it shone like burnished silver. Teams of cleaners on their hands and knees buffed away at it all day long.

It shone like some jewel in a dungeon. In the half-light that passed for daytime in Wandsworth, it shimmered in the gloom like a lake of molten metal. To the screws, it was almost hallowed ground. Amongst the cons, it was known throughout the system as absolutely and totally out of bounds.

Apart from the cleaners, who knelt on cloths, no con's shoe would ever touch it. And if some new reception happened to blunder on to its outermost edges, every assembled screw would scream at him in unison until he retreated.

Only the screws walked on it. In fact it was the central point of the jail and the place where the senior screws congregated. You could always find at least one Chief, a couple of POs and several SOs standing in a group on the Centre.

Often these white shirts would just stand there saying nothing, running their eyes over all who passed. There was something almost reptilian in their total lack of compassion.

The cons had to keep strictly to the pathway when traversing the Centre and then only in a clockwise direction. If you wanted to go from 'E' wing to 'D' wing, you couldn't nip across the dozen or so feet between them, the logical route. You would have to make a complete circuit of the Centre, past A, B and C, in a clockwise direction.

And woe betide any con who had his jacket unbuttoned or his shirt hanging out. It wasn't necessarily a nicking. Just a loud and very public bawling out; the humiliation of a grown man in a tone you wouldn't talk to a dog in. It was far worse than any nicking. And there was always the danger that uncontrollable pride would force you to say something back. Then you would really be in trouble.

Harry was a young fella from Huddersfield. He had come down from the North to try to make it in London. Before long he had turned to burglary. He wasn't particularly professional at it. When they finally nicked him for one, they charged him with the lot. He was found guilty of about 50. He got five years.

He was like a fish out of water in Wandsworth. There was no prisoner power as such, but he quickly saw that the London robbers were the most influential. On exercise and in the workshops he heard them talk. He was thoroughly impressed by their attitude and professionalism. He had never met people like them before.

The majority totally ignored him. To them, he was just some thick Northern burglar who didn't have a clue. At the best of times Londoners were very cliquey. Harry didn't fit the mould at all.

In this he didn't really help himself. There was nothing he could do about his Yorkshire accent, but his general image left everything to be desired. He was dour, unfashionable and scruffy.

Wandsworth was never a fashion parade, but the 'chaps' at least made an effort to look clean and tidy. Through people they knew they would get kit that fitted them. It was possible to have clothes pressed up for wearing on visits. Nothing was more disheartening for a wife or girlfriend than to come on a visit and see their normally immaculate fella done up like a bundle of rags.

Harry was totally oblivious to all this. He didn't get visits, but even if he did style would have been at the bottom of the agenda. None of his clothes fitted. His baggy grey trousers were several sizes too big. He was forever pulling them up from where they had fallen down around his hips. At the bottom they were piled up, concertina fashion, over his shoes.

The shoes themselves were scuffed and dirty. His shirts always had crumpled collars, with several buttons missing. His pride and joy was a large, shapeless grey jumper with holes in it. He was never seen without it. There was a rumour that he even slept in it.

His haircut was unfashionably short at the sides and long on the top. Untidy tufts of fairish hair sprouted in various directions. A long ragged quiff hung haphazardly over one ear. The final touch was added by a pair of National Health glasses, through which he peered owlishly.

Whereas bikers and hippies displayed a deliberate, dishevelled appearance, Harry was just a mess. A fashion consultant wouldn't have known where to start with him and probably wouldn't have bothered. Small wonder that the majority of the London robbers totally ignored him.

A couple talked to him though. He was immediately impressed that, underneath the hard and violent exterior, they were decent, honourable fellas whom he could trust not to take a liberty. On their part, although they largely treated Harry as a joke, they respected the fact that he was staunch and rebellious. They were reasonably certain that he would never grass, and if ever there were a protest against the screws, then he was sure to be there. Also, with all the slippery bastards about, they liked his simple, ingenuous nature.

Harry quickly came to realize what his strong points were in the eyes of the chaps who spoke to him. He played on them to the full. He set out to wind up the screws on the Centre.

Firstly, he greased the long hair on top of his head and combed it straight upwards. In the days of neat, stylish hairstyles he looked like a man who had just had a severe shock. He put on his glasses upside down and set off around the Centre.

The four white shirts standing in a bunch didn't take a blind bit of notice of him. They continued talking amongst themselves, all the time running their eyes over everything. Harry completed the circuit and returned to 'D' wing.

The Londoners who talked to him had been standing there watching. 'I haven't finished yet,' he said as he hurried into his cell.

When he reappeared, his hair and glasses were just the same, but now he had his shoes on back to front, tied on with string. He set out again around the Centre.

Once again, the white shirts did nothing. They continued to talk and look around. The discerning, however, noticed the screws' beady eyes focus briefly on Harry as he passed. They had seen a million nutters though. If they pulled every bizarre-looking fella who passed, the place would grind to a halt.

Harry arrived back on 'D' wing again. He was annoyed that he had been ignored, but at the same time he was relieved. He was enjoying himself. The Londoners were standing there laughing, so his reputation as a rebel was increasing. He could imagine them telling their pals.

'I'll show them this time,' he said as he disappeared inside his cell again.

Within seconds he was back. The hair, the glasses and the shoes were still exactly the same, but this time he had a small hearing aid stuck in his left ear. A thin wire ran from it to disappear down the front of his jumper. Turning to the two Londoners, Harry ostentatiously pulled the wire out. It was only six inches long and obviously wasn't connected to anything. He tucked it back into his jumper and set off for the Centre again.

This time he walked straight out on to the polished grating, heading across it. The white shirts reacted as if struck by an electric current. As one, the four of them screamed at Harry and waved their arms. A short, stocky SO ran at him, his face contorted in rage. 'Get off the fucking Centre,' he screamed.

Harry stopped and looked at him bemusedly. He pointed dumbly at the hearing aid wedged in his left ear. The SO stood and stared, clearly noticing it for the first time. His main weapon had been neutralized. What was the use of shouting at an inmate who couldn't hear you? He could hardly tell him off for walking on the Centre either. And from the way this inmate had just pointed at his ear, he was probably dumb as well as deaf. Any communication with him would be difficult in the extreme. It wasn't worth the trouble.

Dismissing him from his mind, the SO waved Harry away,

back the way he had come. To make his intention absolutely clear, he put one hand on his arm and gently pushed him in the desired direction.

Harry turned away, back towards 'D' wing. He could feel a smile coming, so he twisted his head away from the SO. As he did so, the end of the wire came clear of the top of his jumper and hung there, swinging freely.

The SO stared at the wire, transfixed. Spinning Harry around, he pulled down the front of his jumper. There was no battery pack or anything; the hearing aid was clearly a dummy.

Whilst all this was going on, dozens of pairs of eyes were on them. The three white shirts, still in a bunch, followed every move. Several screws standing about the Centre watched closely. Whenever a screw went to confront a con, anything could come of it.

'Get this man down to E1,' screamed the SO at the top of his voice. Harry stood there paralysed. He was swept up by a tidal wave of blue uniforms that suddenly engulfed him. None of the screws on the Centre had missed a trick. They had seen him walk past in disarray. They had just ignored it. Now he had deliberately walked on their Centre. If he got away with it, everybody would be doing it. There was a lesson to be taught here. It wasn't a mistake either. Clearly, he was taking the piss.

Harry was carried bodily across the Centre by seven screws. With the SO running along behind them, they pushed passing cons out of the way. At a run now, they charged on to 'E' wing. As they headed down the steps to E1, Harry's glasses fell off, followed by one of his shoes.

They rushed him to the end of E1, where the strip cells were. They threw him bodily against a wall. As he landed in a heap on the floor, they kicked at him with their heavy boots and hit him with their sticks.

Dazed and hurt, Harry tried to cover his head with his arms. One particularly stunning blow paralysed him, though, and he felt himself drift away into unconsciousness. The last thing he remembered was the screws tearing at his clothes.

As he lay in a crumpled heap, the screws pulled his clothes off. Those that didn't come easily they ripped to pieces. Then they lifted his naked body by the arms and legs and dumped him in the bare strip cell. They left, slamming the door behind them. It wouldn't be opened until the following morning.

Harry's mind swam back to consciousness. The numbing dizziness was immediately replaced by intense pain. It seemed to be coming from several places at once. He groaned loudly as he rolled over on to his back. Every movement caused his body to scream in protest. Yet no matter how he lay, the pain raged all over him.

He pulled himself up into a seated position and sat hugging his knees. The memory of recent events flooded back to him, and he felt tears well up in his eyes. It was the effects of the pain, coupled with a degree of self-pity. But he couldn't afford to feel sorry for himself. He still had a night to face, naked in the strip cell.

He crawled over to a board in the corner that passed for a bed. There was a canvas sheet folded on it. Ignoring the stains and the accompanying smells, he pulled it around his shoulders. It wasn't much against the cold of the coming night, but at least it might stop him shivering.

Under the sheet he ran his hands all over his body, examining himself for damage. There were several sore lumps, but nothing seemed to be broken. He hugged his knees tighter, trying to warm himself.

It was no use his ringing the bell. If the screws did answer, it would only be to beat him some more. Staring at the featureless walls surrounding him, he felt the loneliness beginning to close in. But, at that moment, it was preferable to any company he was likely to get.

In another corner of the cell he saw a lidless piss-pot next to a plastic water jug. Suddenly he realized he was very thirsty. He crawled over to the jug, praying that there would be water in it. It was half full, but the surface of the water was coated with a dusty film that indicated it had been there for several days. Screwing up his face, Harry took a big gulp. He swallowed it immediately, trying not to register any taste it might have.

He crawled back over to the bedboard; to stand and walk would have been too painful. He lay on his side, covering himself with the sheet. It occurred to him that he was like a wounded animal. This was what the screws had reduced him to.

Strangely the thought strengthened him. They had degraded him, but in the process they had degraded themselves the more. They were supposed to be the forces of law and order. They liked to look down on the convict lawbreakers, thinking themselves to be morally superior. Yet they regularly committed similar offences. The only difference was that they were never pros-ecuted for it. For Harry, this only gave justification to his rebelliousness.

Eventually he must have slept. He woke, cold, stiff and hungry. He lay there for what seemed an hour before the cell door eventually opened. A group of screws stood outside.

'Come on, out you come,' said one. Harry staggered out, blinking in the brighter light. They shepherded him along the 'ones' and into a normal punishment cell. As the door banged behind him, he saw some clothes piled in the corner.

He dressed and sat in a cardboard chair. Half an hour passed, and the door opened. He was served breakfast, but before the door closed again a screw handed him a small printed form. It was a nicking sheet. As Harry read it, he saw he had been charged with assaulting a screw. No doubt that was to cover the assault on himself.

Another 30 minutes passed before his door swung open again. It was the doctor, checking that he was fit for adjudication. Harry looked at the drawn face and tightly pursed lips. This doctor was renowned for his lack of compassion. It would be a waste of time complaining to him.

'Are you OK?' asked the doctor in a harsh, nasal voice. There was no enquiry in the tone. No solicitude or any desire to extract information. It was almost as if he were daring Harry to make a complaint.

Harry just grunted his assent. It was no use his saying anything. He wouldn't be believed anyway. Then he would be charged with making a false accusation as well. It was best to say nothing. The doctor turned and left.

Another hour passed. He heard a lot of movement outside on the 'ones'. Sharp, clipped, military-like shouts echoed around the chokey. Suddenly his door crashed open. A group of six screws stood in the doorway. 'Stand up. Prisoner for adjudication,' one shouted at Harry.

Harry walked to the door. The screws formed up front and back of him. 'Prisoner march,' yelled the same screw. This show of military precision seemed quite funny to Harry. Very different from the undisciplined beating he had received the night before.

He was marched to stand before a table where a Governor was sitting. 'Name and number to the Governor,' ordered the screw. Harry gave his name and number. Hardly looking at him, the Governor read out the charge and told him he would be remanded to appear before the Visiting Committee. 'About turn,' demanded the screw. Almost before he knew it, Harry was back in his cell with the door banged behind him.

The VC was much the same. Two days passed, then he was marched out of his cell again. This time he was taken into a room opposite. It was two cells knocked into one and served as an office. He was marched to stand before a long, wooden table.

Two screws stood directly in front of him to prevent him from jumping over the table. As he peered over their shoulders he could see the magistrates seated there.

There was one old boy with a military bearing. He was sitting very erect with a stern expression on his face. The other three were elderly ladies. Their prim faces and neat but unfashionable clothes reflected their thoroughly middle-class backgrounds. The four of them peered over their glasses to look at the dishevelled Harry, as if he were something the cat had just dragged in.

Once again Harry realized he would be wasting his breath here. 'All I did was walk across their poxy Centre, then they beat me up,' he could imagine himself saying. The magistrates would look at Harry, then at the officers, so smart and military-like, standing to attention in their uniforms. His word against that of several screws. It would be no contest.

Suddenly Harry felt sick of the whole charade. Some justice this. The more he saw of these bastards, the more he felt his rebelliousness to be justified. He just wanted to get it over with and leave the room.

They went through the motions. The charges were read out. The screws gave their evidence. They magistrates peered again at Harry. He was only short and tubby. The officers guarding, towered above him.

'What manner of man could he be that he had attacked six of them?' He read their unspoken question as they stared at him. 'But, then, the place was filled with savages. The officers must have such a difficult job.'

When his turn came, Harry pleaded guilty. He was marched outside whilst they deliberated. Then he was marched back in again. In his best military tone the old gent passed sentence.

'Harry S—— you are sentenced to 180 days' loss of remission and 56 days' cellular confinement. Take the prisoner away.'

Sitting in his cell later, Harry mused on his situation. He had been beaten up; lost six months' remission (the equivalent of a nine-month prison sentence) and faced two months' solitary. All for merely walking across the Centre. The only consolation was that now he was likely to be shipped out when his punishment finished.

'Just think what I'd have got if I'd done something serious,' he said to himself out loud. Shaking his head he tried to smile. But a smile just wouldn't come.

When his 56 days were over, Harry was transferred to Parkhurst. There he was involved in various protests. He lost more remission and served more solitary. In all his time in prison, though, he had never been violent. Those who knew him well would say that it wasn't in his nature.

It is rumoured that when he was released he went back to Huddersfield. Putting into practice what he had learned from listening to the London robbers, he tried to rob a local betting officer with a sawn-off shotgun. An old fella wrestled with him, grabbing the gun. It went off, killing him instantly.

Harry ran out of the shop, with a crowd in hot pursuit. For a while he lost them as he ducked into a church. He reappeared, dressed in the vicar's robes. He was recognized, chased and caught.

At the subsequent trial he was described by the judge as a cold-blooded killer. He was sentenced to life, with a 30-year minimum recommendation.

Those of us who had known him, and his bumbling, harmless ways, were astounded. We knew plenty who fitted the judge's description, in fact, there were some amongst us. But not Harry. We mused on a system that could take a petty burglar and change him so much in the space of only four years.

3. The Treatment Queue

ONE CLASSIC AND enduring image of Parkhurst was the 'treatment queue'. Half-way along the 'ones' on 'A' wing was the treatment room. It was an empty cell lined with shelves and small cupboards. All along these shelves and in the cupboards were various types of medicines. There were glass jars containing liquids of every colour. There were tubs of cream, tubes of ointment and bottles of pills.

Every morning, as soon as 'A' and 'D' wings were unlocked, two hospital screws would appear and unlock the treatment room. They would carry with them a wooden tray with a handle. It contained several bottles of medicines that were too dangerous to leave unattended in the treatment room.

There would always be a couple of fellas waiting outside when the screws arrived. The room had a stable-type door. The screws would push the bottom half shut behind them, then spend a minute or so arranging the bottles on the shelves. Finally, they would turn to the doorway and place a metal bowl and a stack of plastic medicine tots on the shelf on top of the half door. This was the signal that they were ready to start serving.

By now quite a queue would have formed, with more joining every second. Most of them had got straight out of bed. Some would still be in pyjamas, some in trousers and a vest, and a couple in shorts. All were unshaven and thoroughly dishevelled.

Most were on regular medication prescribed by the prison doctor. They would be there every day collecting something. Others would show up when they felt like it and ask for whatever they felt they needed. The screws would hand it out. It was very easy to become a medication junkie at Parkhurst. Almost half the population were on something or other.

As men reached the front of the queue, they would ask for Librium, Valium, Triptycil, Largactyl or some other psycho-tropic drug. A small medicine tot brimming with coloured liquid would be placed in front of them. They would drink it down and throw the empty tot into the metal bowl. Sometimes, men who had built up a strong resistance to one particular drug had a cocktail of tots lined up in front of them.

The medication seemed to have a similar effect to alcohol in that it shut down whole levels of higher thought. Men walked about zonked out for the rest of the day. Unlike alcohol, though, it didn't have an euphoric effect.

The recurring ritual of the treatment queue was repeated just before dinner and again before tea. There was a final treatment call, mostly for sleeping draughts, at about 8 p.m.

Every single day of the year two hospital screws would be there doling out the drugs. Whatever else might be delayed or cancelled, the men always got their treatment. Some were so dependent that there was a good chance they would run amok if they didn't get it.

Such was the volume of traffic to get treatment that there was a separate treatment room for most parts of the prison. 'B' wing and 'C' wing each had its own treatment room, so did the Security Wing. Outside each, queues would form three times a day. A few would ask for cream for a rash or something for a headache. The vast majority requested one or more of the various psychotropic drugs. They were given whatever it took to get them through another day's bird.

4. Wally and the Turds

PARKHURST'S TIN SHOP was far from being an ideal place to work, but there were worse shops. There were about six of our crowd in there now, all staunch people. We managed to have a laugh, but we also knew what work we had to do. So the screws and civvies left us to get on with it.

Fred soon realized that, of the options available to him, the tin shop would suit him best. We realized this, too, and weren't looking forward to him coming in. We wouldn't have done anything to block his chances; you didn't do things like that. However, it was all academic anyway. As an 'A' man and a London gangster, where Fred was concerned, one of the AGs attached to the 'labour board' would make the decision.

The labour board duly sat, and we were all relieved to hear that he had been put in the press shop, the one adjoining ours. Whereas the tin shop, which mostly turned out waste-paper bins, was a labour-intensive production line with a tolerable noise level, the press shop was a Dante's *Inferno* of large, sophisticated machines designed to bend and tear metal. The noise was horrendous.

I never liked the place, often musing on the thought of lunatics operating dangerous machines. I secretly dreaded the day when there would be some terrible 'gavolt', and the medics would cart someone away minus an arm or a leg.

We rarely had need to enter the press shop in the course of our work, and as there was none of our crowd in there we didn't go in for social reasons. We were quite pleased that we wouldn't see much of Fred during working hours.

Fred had other ideas though. He was well aware of the distinct lack of warmth towards him from most Londoners, but he was nothing if not thick skinned. We often joked that you couldn't wound him with an elephant gun.

One of the ways he tried to curry favour with us was to wind up the screws and the civvies. Since we all hated both of these groups, this was a pastime that won him some support. And to give credit where it was due, he could be very funny at times.

It was very difficult to wind up the screws at Parkhurst for the simple reason that they rarely spoke to us, and we rarely spoke to them. And any screw who stood for being wound up, wouldn't have lasted very long.

The civvies, though, were a different matter. In some ways they were in the middle. They had to work alongside us every day and, when necessary, tell us what to do in the most diplomatic way possible. Theirs was an unenviable task.

For the most part they were ordinary working men with a background in engineering. Nothing in their experience could have prepared them for working cheek by jowl with some of the most volatile and dangerous prisoners in the country.

They were given no training in 'control and restraint' techniques, and it was made very clear to them that such things were the sole responsibility of the screws. Consequently, they bent over backwards to avoid antagonizing us in any way. All work directions were in the form of requests. All complaints about us were made as sly phone calls, at which stage the screws would appear and take the initiative.

There were only two civvies in our shop, dry, colourless nonentities whom we treated almost as part of the production process. Relations were always polite and informal, but we never joked with them or otherwise socialized.

In the press shop there were four civvies. They were similarly colourless, but there was one amongst them, a civvy called Wally Pearson, who fancied himself as something of a mover and a shaker. He prided himself that he could keep the press shop running smoothly. That this was done with a mixture of flattery, slyness and general obsequiousness didn't seem to detract from his good opinion of himself.

Pearson was a tall, portly, middle-aged man with the sharp, pointed features of a wary rodent. His thinning black hair was slicked down tight to his head in a passable imitation of the Joe Loss 30s' style. This made him seem all the more sleek and rodent like. All his movements were quick and furtive. He could look you in the eye, but only just.

Not surprisingly he had a reputation for insincerity. He would say one thing to your face, but his real feelings were always delivered by way of behind-your-back phone calls and secret reports. Luckily for our crowd, he rarely came into the tin shop. When he did, he stayed well away from us. This may well have had something to do with the fact that whenever he did appear someone would call out in a loud voice, 'Nitto, chaps! Here's Wally the Rat.'

Pearson must have been warned about Fred. In his own parochial way he must have been totally in awe of him. The fact was that he now had a notorious and feared gangster in his shop. He immediately resolved to be as obsequious as he could.

Pearson made Fred 'shop cleaner'. Cleaning jobs were quite sought after as there was little real work involved. Consequently, Fred just wandered around all day and did next to nothing. The ever present broom was largely a prop to justify his existence.

Pearson also took to calling Fred by his first name. This strategy was absolutely the worst one he could have adopted. Fred always took kindness for weakness. At those times when he wandered into our shop, he would boast about how he had Pearson terrified of him and eating out of his hand. 'You watch me drive him mad,' he promised.

The opening shots in the campaign were comparatively low-key. When Pearson wanted Fred he would call out a demure, 'Fred,' delivered *sotto voce*. When Fred wanted Pearson he would roar out a thoroughly uncouth, 'Wally,' from any part of the press shop.

Fred then got several other cons to do it. Soon the press shop echoed to shouts of 'Wally' between the crashes and bangs of the machines.

Pearson must have been aware that all the familiarity had got out of hand, but once he had set out on the road to appeasement he probably decided that he would have to put up with the consequences. To take the matter up with a Governor now would have got him a rocket for using Christian names in the first place.

The more familiar Pearson got with Fred, the more he bent over backwards to avoid antagonizing him in any way. From observing Fred's manner and antics he was now convinced that he was quite mad as well as dangerous. Pearson would agree with even his most outrageous statements.

Fred took to talking to Pearson about his sister. Now Fred didn't have a sister, but Pearson wasn't to know that. In fact, from the way that Fred went on about her, Pearson was certain that he idolized her. He would listen to Fred emotionally raving about what he would do to anybody who ever insulted or upset his sister in any way. Pearson was no doubt relieved that he would never meet the woman.

One day Fred came into the shop and told Pearson that he had just received a letter from his sister with a photograph enclosed. He asked Pearson if he would like to see it. Realizing that he was on very dangerous ground indeed, Pearson said that he would love to. Fred took the envelope out of his back pocket and reverentially removed a small, black-and-white photo.

Pearson mentally steeled himself as he was handed the picture. However ugly or unattractive the sister might be, Pearson resolved not to say anything that could be remotely construed as derogatory. As he gazed at the face of a blowsy, middle-aged white woman performing fellatio on a large, black penis, Pearson didn't turn a hair. Whatever went through his mind, it didn't show on his face. Pausing as long as he decently could before handing it back, he realized that some remark was required of him. 'She looks like a nice girl, Fred,' he said before discreetly disengaging and hurrying away into his office.

Fred immediately came into the tin shop and told us about it. It really cracked us up. We had been listening to the developing saga and could imagine Pearson squirming whilst Fred kept a straight face. What really provoked our contempt, though, was Pearson's obsequious remark. We all believed in direct and violent action. Pearson's craven behaviour just highlighted for us the dangers of appeasement.

As part of his general plan to appear a nice fella to the cons who worked in his shop, Pearson brought *The Sun* in each day. He would read it at the ten o'clock break, then allow anyone else to read it as long as it was put back in his jacket pocket at the end of the day. He explained that his wife liked to read it over her supper. This arrangement had been going on for several months before Fred arrived.

One morning, as the fellas arrived for work, it was plain to see that Pearson was distressed. His face was grim, and his normal, phony cheeriness was missing. He hurried about, obviously preoccupied with something, as he started the production process going. As soon as he had done this, he called Fred over. They went into the office together and closed the door.

Pearson had originally decided on a strong line, but in the

cold light of day and the presence of Fred his courage deserted him. He settled for sympathy.

'Fred, it was terrible last night,' he whinged. 'I was just getting ready for supper when my wife let out a terrible scream. I ran to the table to find her pointing in horror at the centre pages of *The Sun*. Someone had shit right in the middle and carefully folded it back up again. She was very distressed. Who could have done such a thing?'

Now Fred knew very well who could have done such a thing, for he had done it himself. He had expected this very conversation in fact. For a second he was on the verge of saying, 'Well, you can always expect a lot of shit in *The Sun*,' but thought better of it. A bit of tact was called for.

'Wally,' he said angrily, 'I've got the right fucking hump over this. You're good enough to bring your paper in for us each day, yet some dirty bastard goes and does this. I'm going out into the shop right now and sort it out.'

Fred rushed out into the shop. He hurried behind a large machine and burst out laughing. A crowd of fellas quickly gathered around him. He told them what Pearson had said. They immediately fell about laughing too. He came into our shop and told us, provoking more laughter.

When he returned Pearson was still sitting in the office with the door shut. The shocked and hurt look remained on his face. Fred hurried in without knocking. 'Wally,' he said, 'I've had a word with the fellas, and they're all agreed that it's a fucking liberty. I can't find out who did it, but it won't happen again.'

That was it. Pearson looked at him as if expecting more, but quickly realized that this was all he was going to get. He seemed somewhat mollified, but all this really meant was that he had swapped his shocked look for a sulky one. For the rest of the day he was unusually distant and withdrawn.

• • •

It was late July, and high summer had finally come to the tin shop. We roasted in the unrelenting heat. We opened all the windows and got the screws to open all the doors, leaving just the gates locked. Everywhere was still hot and sweaty though.

In the press shop the temperature was even more oppressive. The machines seemed to blast superheated air into every nook and cranny. Men sat listlessly in any cool corner they could find, but there was no escape from the heat.

Every day, at ten in the morning and three in the afternoon, the shop stopped for tea. A short blast on a siren announced its beginning and end. The cons would huddle in groups over cups of tea or coffee. The civvies retreated into their office to eat the sandwiches and pies their wives had packed for them. They shut the door behind them and forgot about the press shop for the duration of the break.

The four civvies of the press shop shared an office. It was an untidy construction of perspex and metal panelling. The perspex didn't have the clarity of glass, and as the civvies moved about inside their images were blurred like an out-of-focus film.

The office was only about 12-foot square, but it was grossly overcrowded with desks, chairs, lockers and cupboards. Catalogues and paperwork were strewn everywhere. Pearson and his men seemed quite at home amidst all the clutter though. They could be seen nibbling at their sandwiches and chatting amiably.

For Fred, however, this was a state of affairs that couldn't be allowed to continue. It was anathema to him that, for a full 20 minutes each morning and afternoon, Pearson could escape from his influence. He resolved to do something about it.

Firstly, he got several clear polythene bags from the store. He took one into the recess with him and shat into it. Then he tightly knotted the bag at the top. He hid it underneath one of the machines. He then got several other cons to do the same. Fred now had a collection of turds, each preserved in its own polythene bag.

Over the next couple of days he would wander into the office with one of the bags hidden in his pocket. He would pick a time when there was only one civvy in there. Waiting until the civvy was busy writing or distracted by a phone call, Fred would suddenly lean over a big filing cabinet and drop the bag down the back. Then he would amble out again.

Soon there were several turds in bags lying behind the big cabinet. There was no chance of their being found, the office was never properly cleaned. Fred knew this better than anyone. He was the cleaner. To move the heavy filing cabinet would be a major operation, and there was no reason to do so anyway.

Fred left the bagged turds lie there for several days. The bags swelled like balloons as the fetid gases expanded in the heat. The knots kept them sealed though.

Fred had taken to walking about the shop carrying a length of stick, with a nail embedded in the end. He told Pearson it was a 'litter stick', for picking up bits of paper without bending down. Pearson didn't care if Fred walked about with a lance, just so long as he left him alone.

Fred ambled into the office one morning, carrying his stick. It was about 20 minutes before tea-break. As the civvy went to answer the phone, Fred quickly leaned behind the cabinet and punctured all the bags with his stick. He ambled out of the office again and went to join a group of fellas huddled behind the machines. They settled down and waited for the fun to start.

The siren sounded and tea-break started. Pearson and the other three civvies went into the office. Despite the heat Pearson still shut the door. It was a symbolic act, distancing himself from the cons and the shop for the duration of the break.

They settled down in their chairs and rummaged through their bags. They took out their sandwiches and pies and put them on the desks as normal. Pretty soon, though, it was obvious that all was far from normal.

First, the youngest civvy, a slight, fair-haired fella in his late

20s, stood up quickly as if coming to a decision and opened all the office windows as far as they would go. He sat back down again and continued eating. But something was still wrong.

Then Pearson jumped up and ran to the door. He stood in the doorway, swinging it backwards and forwards like a fan. Leaving it wide open, he went and sat down again.

Suddenly an argument broke out. A couple of the civvies were shouting and waving their arms about. Pearson had gone very red in the face and was shaking his head angrily. Fred was too far away to hear what was being said, but, from the gestures, it looked as if someone had accused Pearson of farting.

Equally suddenly, all four civvies rushed out of the office to stand in a group outside. They continued to argue.

Soon, they became aware that all the cons were looking over at them. Even the screw in the observation box had turned to stare at this unusual sight. Self-consciously, they looked at each other. It was a clear choice between abandoning their tea-break or putting up with the smell. They all filed back in.

In the event it was the shortest tea-break on record. For the 15 minutes that remained they ate in silence, all the while frantically fanning sheaves of paper about in an attempt to dispel the stench.

Fred couldn't get into the tin shop quickly enough to tell us about it. It was the climax of his campaign and a telling victory. We all laughed at the stupidity of the civvies for sitting there in the stink, without realizing that something was very wrong. Any con would have recognized the 'shit' smell straight away and suspected a joey.

They were undoubtedly naive, but maybe they weren't suspicious by nature. Perhaps they couldn't conceive that a grown man could do such a thing to them. Whatever the reason, the turds continued to lie behind the cabinet giving off their foul stench.

The civvies avoided going into the office as much as possible now. Phone calls were answered virtually on the run. Break-times were an obvious trial. They took to bringing in air-freshener sprays, but it just made the smell all the more sickly. They rarely took longer than ten minutes for any break now.

Over the weeks, as the turds petrified behind the cabinet, the smell died down. No longer was there the gut-churning stench that would make you want to vomit. There was still a significant smell, but at least it was bearable. Gradually the civvies extended their breaks until they were taking their full 20 minutes again.

5. The Nine Lives of 'Top-cat'

BARRY HARLEY WAS one of the first friends I made on arrival at Parkhurst. He was a ginger-haired ex-fighter, with a mercurial and highly unpredictable temperament. His nickname, 'Top-cat', was largely self-imposed, although he did have much of the arrogance of the cartoon character.

There was little doubt that Top-cat was mentally unbalanced in the first place. The regularity of his violent outbursts stood testimony to that. There was, however, the incident at Wandsworth when several screws had tried to hang him in the punishment block. This probably destroyed any last vestige of his self-control.

Whilst this 'Wandsworth Factor' might have justified Barry's antipathy to screws, it hardly explained his general hostility to everyone else as well. I lost count of the times I talked him out of doing someone because of some supposed slight. I had to take each incident seriously as well, for if I had dismissed it out of hand, he could well have just stormed off and done the fella anyway.

At times it wasn't easy to keep a straight face. One morning he came up to me looking very red in the face and extremely agitated. I immediately recognized the tell-tale signs.

He told me that there was a fella on his landing who he was definitely going to do that very morning. There was much twisting of face and grinding of teeth. He punched his fist into his palm a couple of times.

'What did he do, Barry?' I asked.

He was strangely reticent. Usually he would blurt out the fella's supposed offence. This time I had to drag it out of him.

'I didn't like the way he slopped out this morning,' he admitted sheepishly.

Now as far as I knew, there was only one way to slop out. You took your piss-pot, walked to the recess and threw the contents into the slops sink. The scope for improvisation was minimal.

What had the fella done? A quick pirouette before he chucked the contents into the sink maybe? Perhaps he had approached the sink backwards and thrown it over his shoulder.

No, it was none of these. I finally dragged out of Barry the fact that the fella had thrown the contents of his pot into the sink aggressively, and it had splashed a bit.

I paused to show Barry that I was thinking about it. Then I pointed out two things. Firstly, no doubt the fella was glad to see the back of whatever had been fermenting in his pot overnight. Secondly, the only person he was really going to splash was the person nearest, namely himself. It took some doing, but Barry finally accepted this logic. However, not without a good deal of thought.

There were occasions, though, when there was no time to sit down and rationalize. I was in the gym one morning working out with Eddie from South London and a young giant called Mark. Mark was one of those fellas who had come into prison a skinny teenager and with a combination of regular meals, regular sleep and regular work-outs, had completely transformed himself.

He weighed about 15 stone, had the build of an American quarterback and didn't have a scrap of fat on him. He seemed to grow bigger and stronger by the day. He developed an interest in boxing, and although he didn't have much style he could punch with devastating effect. To see him hit the medicine ball was awesome. In the end there were few people strong enough to hold it for him.

On the debit side he wasn't overendowed with brains and could be a bit flash. He wasn't the best thief you'd ever meet either. He was doing five years for robbing his local butcher, who knew him. Having said that, he had plenty of bottle and could have a fearsome row.

Mark regularly worked out with Eddie and me. This particular morning we were doing some heavy bench press with the Olympic bar. I was 'repping out' with 200 pounds, doing sets of ten.

Mark, however, was repping with 250 pounds for sets of 12 and 15. The massive 20-kilo plates either end of the Olympic bar clanged and jangled as he powered through the sets.

I had just finished my set and was having a breather. Eddie was spotting for Mark. Suddenly a very agitated Barry grabbed me by the arm and pulled me away from the bench. He had been working out on the punch bag, and his face was red and running with sweat.

'Norm, I'm going to do that fucking Mark,' he panted, face twisted, teeth clenched and hands gripped in fists. 'Next time he's bench pressing I'm going to smash him in the face with a twenty. Will you go and stand in the way of the screw's window when I do it?'

I was amazed. This had come completely out of the blue. I had been working closely with Mark and couldn't recall him even so much as looking at Barry. Barry was absolutely adamant though. He was right on the verge of actually doing it.

Now this was no mere punch-up he was talking about. A 20

was an all-steel plate the diameter of a car wheel, which weighed 20 kilos. It would do Mark serious damage to be hit in the face with that whilst laying on his back. Then there was the 250 pounds that he would be holding at arm's length, which would come crashing down on his head. It could easily kill him and would certainly rank as attempted murder.

It would be no problem for me to obscure the screw's view. He was locked in a separate room and could only look out through a small observation slit. That wasn't the point though. There would be a degree of treachery involved on my part, and it wasn't as if Mark had done anything to deserve such an attack.

'Look, Barry,' I said, 'I'm working out with the fella. He ain't a pal of mine, but you can't ask me to do a treacherous thing like that to him. What's he done anyway?'

It transpired that Mark was supposed to have looked at Barry in an aggressive way. In a gymnasium, where everyone was psyched up to get through their workouts, aggression was every-where. It was a measure of Barry's paranoia that he thought Mark's was directed at him.

I managed to talk Barry out of it quite quickly. It was a high-risk strategy, but I just said that I wouldn't be party to it under any circumstances, turned my back on him and walked away to join my workout partners.

Policing Barry was always a hit-and-miss affair though. I couldn't always be there right on cue. There would be times when none of our crowd would be near enough to influence events.

I was standing in the breakfast queue one Sunday morning. I always found it amazing how much the fellas liked their corn-flakes in the nick. Admittedly the normal diet was unrelievedly boring and, more often than not, badly cooked. But if they liked cornflakes that much, I couldn't see why they didn't just buy several packets from the canteen.

Sunday was the one day of the week that porridge wasn't served. You would see people queuing up, who never usually got up for breakfast. Passions could run high. If rations were perceived to be too short, then the screw serving them could expect a volley.

It was a 'touch', a bonus, if someone who wasn't getting up for breakfast said that you could have his ration of milk and cornflakes. Sometimes there was competition between fellas to have this extra ration.

There was a big queue this morning. Barry was about 20 places from the front, and I was several people behind him. I didn't walk forward to join him, because no one pushed in at Parkhurst. There were too many lunatics who might take violent exception.

Barry turned to me and said something jokingly. It was mildly piss-taking, but there was nothing malicious in it. Perhaps it was just too early in the morning for me. I hated queuing up anyway. Stung, I searched for some rejoinder. Something that would sting Barry in return.

Looking past him along the queue, I saw a tall, rangy fella of about 35. He had bright ginger hair. Next to him was his mate, an enormous 17-stone Brummie, who was more fat than muscle. He had an extremely large head, which prompted our crowd to refer to him as 'Pig's Head'. They were both on Barry's landing, and he detested the pair of them. He especially disliked the big, ginger fella (Barry was ginger himself). As usual, I could never find any real reason for it.

However, there was some competition between them to collect the cornflakes of a fella called Brian. At different times, Brian had given them to whoever asked first.

On one occasion, Barry had asked the screw for Brian's ration of cornflakes only to be told that the ginger fella had collected it a few minutes earlier. Barry was still fuming when he spoke to me about it 20 minutes later.

'The big, greedy slag,' he raged. 'If he ever does it again I'll do him.'

This all came back to me as my eyes fell on Ginger. Without really thinking I said, 'Oi, Top-cat. You mind that Ginger doesn't nick Brian's cornflakes again,' and pointed up the queue.

It had an instant effect on Barry. He spun around and peered along the queue. Because of his poor eyesight, he hadn't noticed Ginger before. But he saw him now.

'He'd better not,' he snarled. 'Brian has already said that I can have them.'

I immediately regretted mentioning it. If Barry had already asked Brian, then there shouldn't be any confusion. If Ginger had asked first, then Brian would have told Barry when he had asked for them. Unless, of course, both just assumed that they could have them.

The queue moved on. Ginger collected his breakfast and set off back up to the 'fives'. A minute later, Barry reached the screw who was giving out the cornflakes. Suddenly, I saw them arguing. Barry was instantly very red. He turned to me, pointed upstairs, made a gesture with his fist and mouthed some angry-looking words. Then he stormed away from the queue, up towards his cell on the 'fives' and the direction Ginger had gone.

I realized that, very shortly, it would be off. But I was only half-a-dozen places behind Barry in the queue. I was actually in the process of getting my own breakfast. I couldn't just drop everything and run after him.

Within seconds, I was out of the queue and hurrying towards my cell. I couldn't run because I had on thonged shower sandals, not the ideal footwear in which to have a row. I calculated that Barry would have to drop off his cornflakes at his cell first. I quickly pulled on a pair of trainers, then ran a couple of cells along the landing to get Stewart Down, a close friend of both Barry and me. Ginger and Pig's Head were both big fellas. If there was going to be a row, I might as well have some help.

Stewart jumped up from eating his breakfast and ran out of his cell after me. I only had time to explain briefly. Stewart had started to laugh.

As we ran up the first flight of stairs, we realized that we were already too late. In the distance there was an intermittent rumbling sound. It was the muffled thuds and crashes of two large bodies falling about a small, wooden-floored cell.

It was an instantly recognizable sound. One that might herald dire consequences. It could be a pal who was being attacked. Within seconds you might be involved in a tear-up with knives and lumps of metal.

We increased our pace up the second and third flights. Stewart's expression was serious now. We were both breathing heavily when we reached the 'fives'.

We ran along the landing in the direction of the sound. It had grown louder now. Fellas were stopping on the landing and looking towards the cell. But, at Parkhurst, if it wasn't anyone you knew, then you didn't get involved.

I burst into the cell first. It was a strange sight that met my eyes. Barry and Ginger were locked in combat. There were corn-flakes and milk everywhere. In their hair, clinging to their clothes and all over Ginger's bedspread.

I guessed what had happened. Barry had dropped off his cornflakes at his own cell, then run along to Ginger's. As he ran in, Ginger had been standing up with a bowl of cornflakes and milk in his hands.

Barry must have hit Ginger with a good right hander. You could see the angry red mark on his chin, which was already swelling. The shock and pain showed in his face.

As the punch had gone in, Barry's first must have caught the edge of the bowl. The contents had flown skywards. The welter of cornflakes had risen, only to fall back quickly. Now Barry and Ginger were wearing them like beads in their hair.

You could see that Ginger didn't really want to know. He

was grappling with Barry more in an attempt to stop any further blows than to hurt him. The arrival of Stewart and I only served to reinforce his reluctance. If it wasn't the immediate punch-up that worried him, then it was the heavy come-back afterwards that was his concern. He was looking for a way out.

'Hold up for fuck's sake,' I shouted. There were plenty of things to fight about at Parkhurst, I just didn't think that a bowl of cornflakes was one of them.

Both men continued to cling together. I stepped forward and prised them apart, getting my body between them. As I turned, I noticed Pig's Head standing terrified in the corner. He realized that if it looked like he had been joining in against Barry, then we would steam into him.

I gently forced Barry backwards and, with Stewart's help, got him out of the cell. We led him along the landing towards his own cell. His face was now white with anger. He was definitely in no laughing mood. Stewart, though, was already giggling. To see the usually immaculate Top-cat bedecked with soggy cornflakes was very funny indeed. I started laughing as well.

As we got him into his cell, we saw his own bowl of corn-flakes lying on his table. Turning to us he said, 'Well, he never got to eat the extra bowl, did he?' and burst out laughing himself.

Top-cat liked nothing better than an audience to perform to. The worst thing we could do was to ignore him, and he hated to be left out of anything. Most of the time we did spend with him though. We went to the gym with him, watched TV, went on exercise and ate in the same food-boat. On the odd occasion, however, we would do something he didn't do.

Barry hated cards. He was no good at them and got the hump very quickly. John Harrison, a close friend with whom I ran the racing book, and I both liked a game of kalooki. We both fancied we could play a bit. A lot of the London chaps liked to think they were good at kalooki. Some would play in various London 'spiels'. A lot of money could be won or lost.

John and I were nowhere near that good. John loved a gamble, and I did it for enjoyment. I limited myself to two ounces a week. Once I'd lost that I'd turn it in. And I invariably lost.

We played in a cell up in a corner of the 'fives'. It belonged to a fattish, middle-aged Birmingham fella. He had some kind of stomach disorder, which gave him permanently bad breath. He wasn't one of our crowd, we just played cards in his cell some-times. In our usual irreverent fashion we used to refer to him as 'the Breath'. The card-school was sometimes known as 'the Breath's', but more often as the 'Green Dragon' after a well-known spieler in the East End of London.

On a Saturday evening, especially if we had won a few quid on our racing book, John and I would go up to the Green Dragon for a couple of hours. Big Mick, a giant half-caste pal of ours who was doing 14 years for bank robbery, was always there, Eddie from South London and Brian, he of the disputed cornflakes. The Breath would make a jug of tea, and we would settle down for a quiet Saturday night game of cards and a chat.

This Saturday evening, Barry was over in his cell sulking. We wouldn't have him in the cell with us when we were playing cards. He just couldn't sit quietly. Sooner or later he would have done something and had the whole school in an uproar. Top-cat and cards just didn't go together.

Barry's cell was right across the landing from the Breath's, about 20 feet away. He was tidying up noisily, just to let us know he was there. We pushed the door to and carried on playing. After a while it grew very quiet. We were right up in the far corner of the wing and most people were either up in the 'stage rooms' or down on the 'ones'.

Suddenly there was a muffled crashing and banging from the direction of Barry's cell. It was that sound again, the tumble of heavy bodies rolling about a wooden floor in combat. There were muffled shouts of rage and pain too.

In the Green Dragon, we all froze the moment we heard the rumbling sound. A second or two passed as we looked at each other, deciding if it really was what it sounded like. Then, without saying a word, we all jumped up from the card table and ran across the landing to Barry's cell.

Our faces were tense, our hearts beating faster as increased adrenalin coursed through our veins. We just didn't know what we were running in to. In the crazy world that Barry inhabited it could be anything.

We pushed the door open and crowded into his cell.

Everything was tidy and in its place. There were no signs of the disarray we had expected.

Barry was down on his hands and knees in the far corner. He had his back to us. Shouts and groans came from his direction. He turned to face us, and the noise stopped. He had a large stone in each hand. He had been banging them on the floorboards and shouting, to imitate the sound of a fight.

It had been very convincing, but we weren't amused. We had jumped up from a serious game of cards and run over to what we thought was a heavy tear-up. The adrenalin was still pumping.

As we stood there looking at him, Top-cat suddenly burst out laughing. 'That will teach you to ignore me,' was all he said.

Nothing was ever mundane with Barry. Whatever the situation, he had some little act to stamp his own particular mark on it.

Every weekend we went to the pictures. The show was held in the chapel, up by 'A'-wing 'stage' rooms. It was a serious outing. You could get a couple of hundred fellas there from 'A', 'B' and 'D' wings.

If the film were watchable, it was a good way to escape the boredom for a few hours. The initial settling-down period, though, could be a bit hectic. Fellas would be milling about, speaking to mates from other wings.

Our crowd, a nucleus of born-and-bred London criminals, always sat in a group. We liked each other's company anyway, but it was as much to show solidarity as anything else. There were a lot of dangerous little firms in Parkhurst. We weren't looking for any aggro with anyone, but we wouldn't walk away from it either. What, in effect, we were saying was that if we sat together, we stood together.

Barry would be somewhere in our midst. If he hadn't got a seat with us, there would have been an instant tantrum. He liked to sit next to me. Sometimes, in the scramble for seats, he might end up a couple of chairs away.

We would all get to our places early, talk through the credits, then shut up once the film started. Others, though, would arrive late. Then they would carry on talking through the credits and into the film. They would all shut up eventually, but there could be quite a hubbub for a couple of minutes.

It was very annoying for someone who had come to see the film, but it wouldn't last long. There was little you could do about it anyway. It would have been very dangerous to shout out at particular people to shut up, because, if anyone said anything back, then you would have to jump up and have a row right away. So we let it go.

Barry wouldn't though. The lights would dim. The film would start. But some fellas would still carry on talking. Suddenly, he would scream out at the top of his voice, 'Shut up.'

Now, merely to say 'shut up' hardly does justice to the way that Barry did it. The first part of the 'shut' was a rising scream ending in a shriek. The 'up' was a deep-throated roar, ending in a bellow. The whole thing sounded like a madman who had finally come to the end of his tether and couldn't stand the distraction any more.

It always knifed through the hubbub of chatter and silenced

everyone immediately. Every time it shocked, even those who were expecting it. We would all jump, and Barry would laugh. So would other people who knew him and had heard it before. But it was always dangerous. It could just happen that some week someone would shout something back. Then Barry would have been clambering over seats, trying to get at the fella.

On 'D' wing our crowd used to put hooch down now and again. It would have been no use trying it on 'A' wing. The screws always made themselves very busy and were forever tearing the wing apart, looking for anything illegal. But 'D' wing was much more relaxed.

With hooch, it was almost like a game with our screws. Many of them enjoyed a drink themselves and could understand our wanting one too. Even if they caught you with it brewing, they would invariably make you pour it down the drain rather than nick you. Once you had it in a cell, though, and had started drinking, they would leave you alone. They didn't want a confrontation with several drunken men that could easily lead to a full-scale punch-up.

In return, sensible people policed themselves. If someone got falling down drunk, the others would take him to his cell, put him to bed, make sure he had some fresh water and a sick bucket, then bang him up.

If anyone started to get violent and wanted to smash the place up, the others would calm him down. In general, it was an arrangement that worked quite well. There was no love lost between the screws and the cons on 'D' wing, but there was some degree of live and let live.

I was the brew-master on our firm. Over the years I had learned how to make hooch from various old Paddies and the occasional Italian, for whom it was something of an art.

I had a flair for organization and was clever at hiding things.

With the right ingredients, I could make a passable brew that tasted a bit like gin and orange. I know what they say about only being able to get up to a certain proof with home-brew, but I found that if I kept 'bombing' the brew with more yeast and sugar it could get very strong indeed.

I got together a couple of clean, one-gallon liquid soap containers; a block of yeast from the kitchen; about 12 pounds of sugar and an assortment of fruit.

The first few days were always the worst. The reaction between the yeast and the sugar always generated vast amounts of gas. It was a sickly, sweet smell, reminiscent of rotting fruit, instantly recognizable to con and screw alike.

There were a variety of tricks used to try to disguise the smell, like sprinkling talcum powder about or smearing winter-green over the door jamb. None was very effective. You just had to keep moving the stuff about.

By day the two containers were moved around various cells on the wing. At night, when there was little chance of a cell search, I had them in my cell. I would nurse them gently, keeping them warm by the pipes and occasionally 'bombing' them with extra sugar and yeast. Usually it took about three weeks. This was a reasonable length of time for a good brew.

The nearer we got to the time of drinking, the more nervous we would become about losing the hooch. On this particular occasion I wanted to drink it on Saturday evening. There were rarely searches on a Saturday, and there was no work so we had all day to strain it off and get everything into position. Also, you had all day Sunday to get over the effects.

Big Mick, though, wanted to drink it on the Friday. He didn't want to take the chance of waiting the extra day and losing it. As I was looking after it, however, this time I had my way. Saturday it would be.

Barry agreed to have the party in his cell. It was an ideal place, right up in the corner of the 'fives'. We would be out of the way, and the screws wouldn't hear too much noise. At least, that was the theory.

It was a brave decision on Barry's part for several reasons. Firstly, you could always count on plenty of mess at a hooch party. Fellas would knock things over and occasionally spew up. Once the hooch hit you, these things could become unavoidable. Barry had a nice, tidy cell that he took a pride in. We all swore we wouldn't mess it up.

The second danger was that, should there be any trouble, you could hardly leave the party if it was in your own cell. Bearing in mind the volatile people who would be attending, trouble was always a distinct possibility.

We were all pals and rarely rowed amongst ourselves. However, we still promised Barry that we'd be on our best behaviour. It was quite a novel situation, with us promising to behave whilst Barry acted the responsible one.

Saturday arrived. I strained the hooch and took it up to Barry's cell. I poured it into a clean, two-gallon plastic bucket and left it in a cool corner. As soon as we were unlocked that evening, our crowd was to make its way up to Barry's cell, and the party would start.

The doors were unlocked at six o'clock, and I climbed the stairs to Barry's cell. It was all laid out ready. The bucket of hooch was in the middle with the lid off. On a nearby table stood several half-pint china mugs. Next to them were a couple of plates bearing neatly made sandwiches. His record player was playing softly in the corner. Barry had clearly gone to considerable trouble for us.

I arrived first, closely followed by Big Mick and Stewart. Then Eddie came in with Mick, a prolific and well-respected robber out of North London. There was a lot of laughing as we greeted each other. Stewart was especially tickled by the sight of Barry playing the serious, if genial host. We took our seats and settled down to wait for John.

About five minutes later he hurried in. He was lucky to be there, because he lived on 'A' wing. He had been trying to move on to 'D' wing for weeks, but the screws wouldn't let him. They didn't like to let too many of us get together on the same wing. On this occasion, though, Eddie had asked our SO if John could come on the wing for the evening. Much to our surprise, he agreed.

The atmosphere was just like a party outside, minus the women of course. Everybody was in good spirits and looking forward to a break in the usual monotony. You had to have these breaks, these high points, otherwise life was all boredom and gloom.

We each took a china mug. Barry filled a jug from the bucket and topped each one to the brim. The golden-orange liquid had just a trace of effervescence on top. The slightly nauseous smell of the brewed fruit made our noses wrinkle.

We had no time for those who would gingerly sniff the brew, though, then sip it. We observed the tradition of the 'first cup'. Holding our breath, we said, 'Cheers,' then drank the whole cupful straight down. No doubt the rush of alcohol to the brain was responsible for much of the drunkenness caused by hooch. It also helped you get used to the rather sickly smell.

I experienced an extraordinarily sweet taste all down the back of my throat. I shuddered involuntarily as the alcohol hit my stomach. Then, an ever growing, warm sensation suffused my whole body.

In no time at all the party was in full swing. The music was blaring, and everyone was laughing and shouting at the top of their voices. We had almost forgotten that we were in prison.

Top-cat was in his element. He had a captive audience and could show off to his heart's content. He told all his old jokes and ran through several of the incidents we had been involved in. It all seemed very funny now. We laughed and laughed.

In a spirit of peaceful coexistence, someone suggested we

invite in a couple of the Jocks for a drink. There were a lot of Scots fellas at Parkhurst, and, on the whole, they were staunch people. The Londoners and the Jocks got on quite well. There was some rivalry, and we moved in different firms, but there was a degree of mutual respect. (At this time it was the epitome of success for a Scottish criminal to come down to London and make it.)

John went out and came back with Hughie and Jamie, two Jocks in their late 20s. At first, they were ill at ease, but after a couple of drinks they were laughing and joking with the rest of us. We were all very drunk by now.

From time to time people would wander off. They went to have a piss, to clear their head or just to stretch their legs. Those less drunk would regularly go out and tour the landings to make sure that one of our crowd wasn't lying drunk somewhere.

Suddenly, I realized that Stewart was missing. I still felt responsible for him. If anything had happened to him, I wouldn't have been able to face his brother, Ian, who was doing 25 years in another jail and who was also a close friend of mine.

Before tea, I had taken pains to ensure that Stewart was prepared for the evening to come. I explained how, after drinking hooch, it was very easy to spew up. It often came after you lay down and the room started to spin around.

I took him into my cell and showed him how I had laid it out. There was a new, plastic washing bowl on the floor beside the bed. A clean towel lay next to it. I explained that if you were sick you would need to drink lots of water. I had a jugful on my table. These were all the things that an experienced hooch drinker needed to know, I had told him.

I left Barry's cell looking for Stewart. I wasn't too steady on my feet myself. I staggered along the landing to the recess, thinking that he might have gone for a piss. As I drew close, I could see some movement in the gloom.

South London Eddie and Mick had a mop each. They were

dancing with them in the recess. I had never seen anything so ridiculous in my life. Here were two of London's better-known villains acting really foolishly. But that was what the hooch could do to you. It was all harmless fun really. Part of it was laughing the next day at the way you had made fools of yourselves the night before.

I carried on looking for Stewart. The stairs down from the 'fives' had never seemed so steep. I clung on to the hand-rails with both hands. As I staggered down each flight, I stopped only to look in each recess. There was no sign of Stewart.

There were no screws about either. Once they had heard the noise of the party and realized who was involved, they had come down from the landings and retired to the relative safety of the office.

Finally, I reached the 'ones'. I staggered across to Stewart's door, only to find it locked. I looked through his spy-hole and could see him lying in his bed fast asleep. Clearly, he had had enough for the evening.

I suddenly realized that so had I. My cell was just across the landing. Before I knew it I was inside and banging the door behind me.

Back at the party things were getting a bit out of hand. John and drink were like fire and gunpowder, a volatile combination. He was falling down drunk by now and had started throwing playful punches. He was a powerful fella, though, and a playful punch from John could hurt. Especially when he was off balance and his timing was out.

Within no time at all he had not only punched Big Mick on the chin but both of the Jocks as well, laughing helplessly all the while. Tempers were becoming frayed. Already pride had been hurt. Luckily, it was nine o'clock, and time for John to get back to his own wing.

As Eddie had been responsible for bringing him over, it was his job to get him back. He steered him out of Barry's cell on the long journey down to the 'ones'. With Eddie leading him, John partly walked, partly fell down the three flights of stairs.

By now it was just after nine. The door through to 'A' wing was open, and a reception committee of 'A'-wing screws was waiting.

'Hold up. Look at these slags,' said John, laughing hysterically. He went into a fit of continuous laughter. He stood in the middle of the 'ones' and wouldn't move. With Eddie pulling on one arm and the 'A'-wing screws shepherding him along, but not touching him, they gradually got him into 'A' wing.

Finally, they pushed him into his cell and banged him up. John was still laughing uproariously. The screws, though, definitely weren't amused. Any chance he had ever had of moving on to 'D' wing was now gone.

When I awoke the following morning, the first thing I became aware of was a terrible stench. It smelt like a combination of all the most loathsome things imaginable. The second thing I noticed was that the side of my face, where it touched the pillow, felt wet and sticky.

I gingerly lifted my head from the pillow. The room spun before my eyes. Looking around, I could see that I must have been sick as I lay asleep. On one side there was vomit all over the pillow and up the nearby wall. On the other I had missed the bed completely and been sick on the floor.

I levered myself up on to my elbows so that I could see more of the cell. Blurry eyed, I saw the new plastic bowl, still where I had put it the evening before. But there was something in it. It was a brown bowl, and whatever was in it was of a similar colour. Suddenly, the smell hit me, the very distinctive smell of shit. Next to the bowl, lying on the floor, was the clean towel I had so carefully laid out. It had a long, brown smear on it.

I cringed as I realized what must have happened. As I had banged my door the night before, I must have suddenly realized that I wanted a pony very urgently indeed. My pot was on the other side of the bed, which I had across the cell. I needed to climb over the bed to reach it. No easy task for someone who was falling down drunk and on the verge of an imminent bowel movement.

I must have realized that I wasn't going to make it in time. I didn't remember dropping my trousers; shitting in the bowl and wiping my arse on the towel before I climbed into bed, but I must have done it, because the evidence was all there before me.

I couldn't believe it. I considered myself to be a very clean-living fella. I was extremely scrupulous about personal hygiene. My cell was always clean and tidy, and I never, ever, shit in my pot.

I felt very embarrassed. I felt even more so when I realized that the night screw must have looked through my spy-hole to check that I was in. Heaven knows what he made of the bowl of turds and the towel with the skidmark. He must have thought I was an animal.

My immediate problem was to get rid of the bowl and its contents without anyone seeing it. I would obviously have to empty it down the slops sink. The trouble was that, first thing in the morning, everybody else was throwing something down there too.

Right next door to me lived a little raver called Jeff. If he saw me slopping out with shit in my washing bowl, you could bet your life that it would be all over the nick by dinner-time. But I couldn't hang about too long, because it stank. Anyone coming in would smell it.

As my door was unlocked, I went straight to the recess with my water jug on a dummy run. Sure enough, there were dozens of people about. I emptied the old water from the jug and filled it with fresh.

When I got back to my cell, I poured some of the water into my empty piss-pot. I went over to the khazi and emptied that.

By now, the early rush was thinning. I went back to my cell and hovered in the doorway. Suddenly there were only people going away from the recess, no one was on their way to it. I dived into my cell, grabbed the bowl and walked quickly to the slops sink. I was committed now; I couldn't turn back.

It went sweet as a nut. Straight into the recess, down the sink, a quick rinse of the bowl, which was then thrown underneath, and I turned around and walked out again.

Later that morning we all met at Barry's. He was cursing the state of his cell. There were dog-ends everywhere, split hooch and a smashed cup. For once, he had been on his best behaviour. It was the rest of us who had acted like fools.

We laughed at Mick and Eddie for dancing with the mops. We jokingly chastised John for setting about people. He wouldn't be allowed on the wing now, and we had to contend with all the Jocks walking about with long faces.

We mocked Stewart for slipping away early and going to bed. In fact, we laughed at all the foolish things that people had done under the influence of the hooch. Except, of course, the foolish thing I had done. But that was because no one had seen mine.

6. The Mackerel

BERT JOHNSON OCCUPIED a strange position amongst Londoners. In general he was thoroughly disliked and kept on the fringes. On the other hand, though, because of his association with the Twins, an effort was made to keep up appearances. It was nothing to do with the fact that Ron and Reg might get the hump if we turned against him; their contempt for him was well known. It was more to do with maintaining the fiction of a united and interlocking firm of London 'chaps'.

There were two main reasons for Bert's unpopularity. The first centred around his case. Although the Twins themselves were widely feared and respected, as were some of their firm, it was common knowledge that they had several hangers-on with them. The latter weren't feared or respected for themselves. They only got away with what they did because people knew they had the Twins' backing. Bert was one of these.

What really upset people and aroused their contempt, though, was Bert's involvement over Jack 'the Hat' McVitie. Whatever people thought of 'the Hat', and he could be a nasty piece of work when he wanted to, it was known that he and Bert were friends and went about together. That was why the Twins told Bert and his brother to bring Jack to the party they had arranged.

As game and as crazy as Jack could be, it was highly unlikely that he would have gone alone. He already suspected that Ronnie had the hump with him. Bert asked Jack along, though, well knowing that Jack must be in for a good beating. In the event he was murdered. There was an 'in' joke amongst the 'chaps' that went: 'If Bert ever invites you to a party, don't go!'

In jail he did little to improve his standing. Most of the 'chaps' were proud men, who tried to conduct themselves with as much honour and dignity as they could. Not Bert though.

He could, however, be very funny at times and regularly took part in various protests. He did his bird easily enough, and you never heard him whining about parole. Nevertheless, he was forever involved in tricky moves and unscrupulous dealings. He just couldn't be trusted.

Amongst our crowd he was known as 'the Mackerel', which is an unflattering term for someone who is slippery and under-handed. He wasn't part of our crowd, although he did come into our company quite regularly.

I personally had the hump with him over an incident at the Scrubs. He had been in the chokey with a fella who died under suspicious circumstances. It was alleged that the screws had beaten him up, accidentally killed him and had then tried to cover it up.

There was intense bad feeling about it in the jail. About 300 of us long termers on 'D' wing had held a sit-down protest. A headline in the local paper read: DID WARDERS MURDER THIS MAN?

At the subsequent inquest, Bert gave evidence that helped the screws out of a tight corner. There was some doubt about the truth of what he said. One particularly radical magazine, *Up Against the Law*, castigated him in no uncertain terms. If he had come back on to 'D' wing, the fellas would have done him. Instead he had been transferred to Parkhurst.

When I arrived, he had hurried up to assure me that his role at the inquest had been exaggerated. I also found that he had already been accepted by some of the fellas. So, having no hard evidence with me, I decided to let it go for the time being. However, I had arranged for a copy of *Up Against the Law* to be sent to me. When it arrived, I was going to confront him with it in front of the fellas. As things turned out, I never got the chance.

Returning to my cell early one afternoon, I found Stewart and Ralph Baron, a friend and founder member of our firm, waiting for me. I could see that something was up by the serious expression on the face of the usually mischievous Stewart. Ralph, too, seemed on edge.

'Norman,' said Ralph, 'we'd like to ask you something.' He nodded to Stewart, who continued.

'Look, Norm,' he said apprehensively, 'just after dinner I went to slop out. As I came out of the recess, I saw Bert going into my cell. We've been playing a few jokes on each other lately, so I ducked back into the recess to watch what happened. After about thirty seconds he came out again and hurried away. I was convinced he had set some kind of silly trap for me.

'I hurried back to my cell and crept inside very carefully. There was nothing on top of the door, and I couldn't find anything else that was wrong. So I forgot about it and carried on having a clear-up.

'For some reason, about half an hour later, I decided to check on that two ounces you gave me to look after.' Stewart paused as if he was coming to the bit he found distasteful. I inwardly cringed, knowing exactly what he was going to say.

'I looked on my bookshelf, behind the books,' he continued, 'and it was gone. It was there before dinner, and no one else had been in. So I don't know what could have happened to it ——'

'We know it's a bit strong,' said Ralph butting in, 'but you know Bert better than we do. Do you think he could have taken it?'

There was an awkward, embarrassed silence as the three of

us stood there looking at each other. This was a very serious matter. Of all the sins that a man can commit in prison, to steal off another con is regarded as the lowest of them all. The presence of nonces and even grasses can sometimes be tolerated, but cell-thieves are usually attacked on sight.

With all the various types of criminal at Parkhurst, nothing ever went missing out of cells. You could, quite literally, leave ounces of snout on your bed with the door wide open, and it would all still be there when you came back hours later.

It was a question of honour. We were all in the same boat. It would be a very weak man who stooped to stealing off other cons just because he was short of a smoke.

Having said that, there was a very severe sanction against cell-thieving at Parkhurst. Rumour had it that a cell-thief had been caught several years previously. The fellas had bashed him, then stuck his hand in the hinged side of a cell door and slammed it. It is said that he lost several fingers.

As much as I would have liked to condemn Bert out of hand, this was something that could utterly destroy his reputation and make him an outcast wherever he went. And there was no conclusive evidence. No one had actually seen him take the snout. Too many people were doing big bird over inconclusive evidence. We often railed against the system because of this. We would be the worst of hypocrites if we judged Bert on similar inconclusive evidence.

'Look, Stewart,' I said, 'firstly, don't worry about the snout. It's only from the book, and we've got about a hundred ounces lying about. Secondly, don't feel embarrassed in any way. It's not your fault. And lastly, yes, I do think he could have taken it, but we've got no real proof.'

I paused to let that sink in. In the back of my mind I was also thinking that it wouldn't look very good to have one of the London firm exposed as a cell-thief. The various firms of Scouses, Jocks and Paddies would all be laughing at our expense.

I decided to tell Stewart and Ralph about the Scrubs incident. I explained briefly.

'I'm only waiting for a copy of *Up Against the Law*, and then I'm going to confront him with it in front of all the fellas,' I continued. 'I'll do it in the khazi on the compound, then we can all steam into him. That will be the last we'll see of the slag. So, in the meantime, let's keep it to ourselves.'

Stewart and Ralph nodded in agreement. As an afterthought I added, 'And, for fuck's sake, don't tell Barry about this.' Barry detested Bert. He refused to speak to him and had been looking for an excuse to chin him for ages. On several occasions I had stopped him from doing him.

Stewart and Ralph both seemed satisfied with what had been said. They walked off towards 'A' wing.

At tea-time, I wandered across to Dave Bailey's cell, which we had come to refer to as the 'Old Bailey'. Dave, a bank robber and one of the leading lights of our London crowd, was sitting there as usual, with both Ralph and Barry. Barry looked very agitated and red in the face. Ralph looked flushed, and Dave had turned his customary 'whiter shade of pale', as he always did when it was off.

'I've done the slag,' said Barry with absolutely no preliminaries. Ralph then explained what had happened.

He had been telling Dave and Barry about the incident involving Stewart's missing snout. He had just finished when Bert walked in. Barry immediately jumped up and steamed into him. As he punched him into the corner of the cell, Ralph ran over and joined in.

Bert fell to the floor and cowered in the corner. 'What's the matter? What have I done?' he shouted. He started to cry.

Ralph and Barry pulled him to his feet. As Ralph threw him bodily out of the door, Barry kicked him up the arse.

For once no one was laughing in the aftermath of the violence. It was no laughing matter. We weren't animals who turned on each other for little or no reason. Although, strictly speaking, Bert wasn't one of our crowd, he was on the fringes. He was also a Londoner. Apart from any other considerations it wouldn't look very good for our solidarity in the eyes of the various other firms.

It could also cause trouble within our group. One of our friends had known Bert since they were kids and quite liked him. Nobody else did, but that didn't mean that they would agree to convict him on wholly circumstantial evidence. There could be a falling out amongst us, and there were enough potential enemies about without that.

Luckily for all concerned, though, Bert's low-life nature saved the day. He had gone straight from Dave's cell to the wing office and put himself on Rule 43. Now, whatever the circumstances, he had damned himself. No one of any merit would ever go to the screws and ask for their protection. The mere act of putting himself on 43 had made him a 'wrong 'un'.

We didn't see Bert again. He was down the chokey on the landing with all the nonces and grasses. It was an embarrassing subject for us, so we didn't even talk about it. After a few weeks we heard that he had been shipped out. We were glad to see the back of him.

7. Baron Blunt

RALPH BARON WAS the rudest man you would ever meet in your life. It wasn't just that he didn't suffer fools gladly, Ralph didn't suffer fools at all. And if a fool ever came within insulting distance, he would soon feel the rough edge of Ralph's tongue.

Rudeness was commonplace in prison. Single-handedly, though, Ralph had elevated it into something of an art form. This was why we called him 'Baron Blunt', a play on his surname.

Ralph was just starting a ten. He had been a prolific bank robber, working with some of the best London firms. At 20 he had been the youngest man ever to be sent to Dartmoor. In those days it was seen as the end of the line for hardened, recidivist criminals.

Ralph was shortish, a bit overweight and in his late 20s. His skin was quite swarthy so that he tended to resemble a Cypriot or someone from Mediterranean climes. He also had a riotous mop of bushy, black hair. Stewart once called him 'Sooty' as a joke. This was about the only time we ever saw the usually imperturbable Ralph lose his cool. The mischievous Stewart never called him that again.

Ralph was highly intelligent and knew it. At times this made him quite arrogant. However, he was witty, funny and very good company. We all liked him.

Ralph was a classic elitist. If you were a London robber with impeccable criminal credentials, then you were OK. If you weren't, then he wouldn't stand you at any price. And he would tell you to your face too. In a criminal subculture that was riddled with hypocrisy, Ralph was like a breath of fresh air. He had his enemies, but these were usually people who had something to hide.

My earliest memory of Ralph was of a day shortly after I had arrived at Parkhurst. I was standing on the 'ones' with Dave, just outside the 'Old Bailey'.

Dave was talking to Kevin, a fella who used to bring him his laundry. Kevin was a big, easygoing Londoner, with close-cropped blond hair. He was only 22, yet had a massive body-builder's physique. He was quite slow-witted, bordering on the thick and was doing a five for a robbery that had been sheer stupidity.

There was no harm in him. He would always do you a good turn rather than a bad one, and there had never been any sugges-tion that he was a grass. However, he totally lacked any professionalism in the pursuit of crime. Perhaps that was why he looked up to the members of our group with a childlike awe.

Dave was just thanking Kevin for some clean laundry he had delivered, when Ralph swept up. He walked right in amongst the three of us and took Dave by the arm.

'Dave,' he said, nodding towards Kevin, 'he's a nice fella, but he's a right fucking bore. If you stand for him now, he will be round every five minutes driving you mad. So the best thing is to blank him right from the start.'

With that, he pulled Dave by the arm and led him away. I was left standing there with Kevin, speechless and not a little embarrassed.

This was classic Baron Blunt. I suppose that someone else might have discretely pulled Dave aside and told him that if he encouraged Kevin at all, then he could become a pest (as we later found out he could be). Ralph, though, chose to be direct. It was a bit cruel, but this was Parkhurst. The message was that mugs could get you into trouble.

At times, Ralph could be a trifle too direct. He had been

looking after two ounces for John and I. Running the book meant that we always had to have 60 or 70 ounces of snout spread about. You were only allowed to hold up to $2^1/_2$ ounces, so we obviously couldn't keep it all ourselves. Consequently we spread it around friends and people we knew. Ralph didn't smoke, so he had no snout of his own. He agreed to look after two ounces for us until we needed it.

Ralph occasionally talked to a black fella called Jay. I assumed that Ralph tolerated him for his intellect. He was an educated man, with a courteousness bordering on the unctuous. For that reason I was always uneasy about him. There was nothing I could put my finger on, but, deep down, I didn't trust him.

Jay was doing life with a 15 rec. He wasn't a robber, but black robbers were very rare in those days anyway. It was an unusually heavy sentence for a black man of his intellect. I wondered what his crime could be that it had attracted such a severe sentence.

Ralph lived on 'A' wing, the wing next to ours. As he walked along the 'threes' with the two ounces I had just given him, he passed Jay, who was talking to another black fella called Jackson.

Jackson was one of those fellas who I hadn't really noticed before. He was very tall and thin. He weighed about 12 stone, but spread out over his six-foot two-inch frame it didn't seem to go very far. He looked all arms and legs. He was a Brummie, doing 15 years for a series of minor armed robberies. In Parkhurst terms, he was a nobody.

I had seen him in the gym a couple of times. In shorts and vest he looked even skinnier. He would punch the bag and clearly didn't have a clue. He held his hands down around his waist and swung wildly. He looked a right wally, but, as they say, punching the bag and fighting are two completely different things.

Ralph passed the pair of them, but only spoke to Jay. He carried on, up to his cell. He had been there about ten minutes when Jay knocked and came in. He told Ralph that, after he had walked past, Jackson had said that he would have to slip in and nick the two ounces.

Perhaps someone less headstrong might have pondered the feasibility of Jackson telling an acquaintance of Ralph's that he was going to rob him. Maybe Ralph should have confronted Jackson and challenged him over it. Unfortunately, though, it was too late for that. The persona of Baron Blunt had sprung into action.

It was early afternoon, and Jackson had just got into bed for quick nap. Suddenly the door burst open and in ran Ralph. In his hand he had a PP9 battery inside two woollen socks. As Jackson raised his head from the pillow, Ralph struck it a stunning blow. It was quickly followed by several more until Jackson lay unconscious in his bed. Then Ralph ran out again, banging the door shut behind him.

When we came in from work at tea-time, the talk was all of Ralph bashing Jackson. If anyone thought that Ralph had gone a bit strong, nothing was said to that effect. We didn't know the full strength of what had gone on. If Ralph were defending the snout we had given him to hold, then he was completely in order. And whatever the circumstances, our group would stand by him. But Baron Blunt certainly hadn't wasted any time in taking direct action. There was a lot of laughter about the incident.

By the following morning it was all largely forgotten. Jackson wasn't particularly dangerous, and he had no help worth mentioning. So Ralph wasn't worried by a come-back. That was where the strength of the group was so valuable to us all. Everyone would think long and hard before making a move against any one of us, well knowing that they would have all the rest of the group to contend with as well.

We weren't bullies. We didn't take anything off anyone. We didn't bother anyone who didn't bother us. But a threat against one was a threat against all.

When we came in from work that dinner-time, you can imagine our surprise to hear that Jackson had bashed Ralph.

We immediately went off to find out how badly he had been hurt. Several of us climbed the stairs of 'A' wing and crowded into his cell.

Ralph was sitting on his bed, more embarrassed than hurt. He had a black eye, which, because of the swarthiness of his skin, didn't look as bad as it might have done. He had also hurt his leg. This didn't explain his bandy-legged gait though. On pressing him further he confessed that Jackson had kicked him in the balls and that they were sore and swollen. The major injury, though, was to his reputation and, by association, to ours too. We asked him what had happened.

Ralph had been walking along one of the landings that morning, when he saw Jackson coming the other way. As he drew close, Jackson stopped.

'Ralph, why did you do that to me?' he asked animatedly. 'What's it all about?'

'I've got fuck all to say to you,' said Ralph dismissively. 'If you've got anything at all to say about it, we can go into the recess and sort it out.'

The wing was all but deserted. Most of the fellas were out at work. Those who were on the wing were sitting in their cells.

'OK, Ralph,' said Jackson, 'after what you've done to me maybe that's the best thing we can do.'

Jackson walked into the nearest recess, and Ralph followed him. Ralph's brother had a black belt in karate. Ralph had done a bit himself but had only achieved a novice grading. I had seen him in the gym, doing a karate workout on the punch-bag. As Jackson shaped up boxing style, Ralph assumed the 'kiba dachi' position, standing square on to Jackson, feet wide apart with his knees bent.

The next thing Ralph remembered was waking up on his bed. Jackson was sitting in a chair beside him.

'What happened?' asked Ralph groggily.

'I knocked you out, man,' said Jackson.

With that, Ralph launched himself off the bed to attack him. He was still weak from being knocked unconscious, though, and his legs crumpled beneath him. Jackson pushed him away and ran out of the cell.

As Ralph finished telling the story, I saw Stewart out of the corner of my eye trying hard not to laugh. To be honest, I felt like laughing myself. I could imagine the situation.

Ralph letting Jackson go into the recess first was mistake number one. The recess was quite dark, with just a tiny window behind Jackson. Ralph had the lights of the wing behind him and would have had trouble seeing the black man in the dark. Jackson would have had no such problem. Ralph was a perfectly lit target.

Ralph's second mistake was to shape up karate style by assuming 'kiba dachi'. If Jackson had realized that it was karate, he clearly wasn't impressed. He promptly kicked Ralph in the balls as hard as he could. The rest was history.

Apart from Ralph's injuries, the immediate problem was that Jackson couldn't be allowed to get away with it. Irrespective of what personal revenge Ralph wanted to take, we wanted our revenge on Jackson for doing one of our group.

It was personal pride, but it was also to do with reputation. There were undoubtedly quite a few who would like to make a move against one or other of our group. But the sanction of an immediate come-back from the rest of us, ensured our individual and collective safety. Jackson had to go.

After we were unlocked for association that evening, John, Barry and Stewart came to my cell. Barry was absolutely champing at the bit. He couldn't wait to get at Jackson. We weren't going to wait to see what Ralph was going to do. Anyway, he was still injured. We loaded up with a couple of blades and a short iron bar and set off for 'A' wing.

The major difficulty was that we were going on to another wing. It wasn't an insurmountable problem, because John lived on 'A' wing and had got across to us. He had walked through the door on the 'ones' when it was opened to allow us through for 'stage'. It was locked again now, though, and wouldn't be opened again until eight o'clock. There was another way, however.

Up on the 'fives', there was an eight-foot partition, which separated the two wings. We often used to climb over it to go visiting. The screws knew about it, but it wasn't a major security hazard. We were only going from one wing to another.

The four of us climbed the stairs to the 'fives'. Most of our wing screws were down in the office. Those that were on the landings were unsighted for the 'fives' partition.

John and Barry lifted me up, and I poked my head above the partition. I peered into the gloom to see what screws there were about. They were very conscientious on 'A' wing and tended to stand on the bridges. This gave them a commanding view of all the landings.

The bridges were clear, though, I couldn't see any screws at all. As I ran my eyes quickly along the landings. I couldn't see any screws there either. But a movement caught my attention. Then I saw them. There must have been a dozen dark-blue uniforms, standing well back in the shadows of the cell doorways. They were obviously waiting for us.

The screws had heard what had gone on between Jackson and Ralph. They had guessed there would be a come-back from us and knew it would be heavy. Perhaps Jackson had told them himself. He couldn't have been under any illusions about what was bound to happen.

There was nothing we could do for now though. John and Barry lowered me to the landing, and we all returned to my cell. We resolved to get Jackson on the exercise yard the following day.

At exercise time the next day all four of us were plotted up in the compound, waiting for Jackson to come out. The screws only stayed on the perimeter, so if Jackson came into the crowds of cons milling about in the centre, then one of us could slip up and do him.

The compound quickly filled up. Soon there were over 200 cons running, walking, sitting, standing or playing games. Many of them had heard about the incident with Ralph and guessed there would be a come-back. There were some knowing looks as we loitered about.

Suddenly, Jackson appeared at the compound gate. He came just inside, then stopped. He stood no further than six feet from the bunch of screws by the gate, and that was as far as he was going. Clearly we had to think up another plan.

The obvious choice was in the cinema. On Saturday night a couple of hundred cons would be crammed into the old chapel up by 'A'-wing 'stage' rooms, to watch the film. Quite a few people had been done once the lights went out. You could crawl along the floor between the rows of chairs, do the business and, by the time the lights went on, be long gone. The cinema at Parkhurst was a very dangerous place.

That Saturday evening all our crowd went to the cinema. By now it was common knowledge that we were going to do Jackson. Those who hadn't been told that something was up could have guessed from the way that Jackson now went everywhere accompanied by two screws. That, in itself, was something of a face-saver for us.

We got to the cinema early and sat in a row near the back. This gave us a commanding view over the rows of tiered seats.

The place rapidly filled up, and within 15 minutes there were 200 people in their seats. Right at the very end, just as they were about to lock the door, in came Jackson accompanied by two screws. The three of them walked right to the back and sat down underneath the projector, with their backs against the wall. Darkness or no, Jackson was safe for another evening.

By now, we were becoming thoroughly frustrated. It seemed that Jackson was being minded all the time. Short of walking up and doing him in front of the screws, there was nothing that could be done.

We also had the added annoyance of Ralph insisting that it was his row and that he was going to do Jackson himself. We were all for that, but we didn't want to get to a situation where it went on and on until Ralph left it. With us, at least we knew for sure that it would be done eventually.

Finally we agreed to let Ralph have the first shot. It was no major concession, because no one could get close to Jackson at the moment anyway. However, we knew that the screws wouldn't keep it up indefinitely. They would tell Jackson either to go on Rule 43 or take the consequences.

Now that the ball was firmly in Ralph's court, he came to my cell early one morning and asked what I would use if I were going to do Jackson.

'It depends how much damage I wanted to do,' I said, looking at him closely. Ralph wasn't in my position. He would be going home in a couple of years. He didn't need to miscue and land himself with a life sentence or another lump of bird on top.

I could see from Ralph's manner that he would be satisfied with just knocking Jackson unconscious and putting him in the hospital for a few days. So all that Ralph would need was a cosh of some kind.

It would have to be small and easily concealable so that Ralph could walk about with it on him. But it would also have to be meaty enough to do some damage. Ralph seemed enthusiastic about the cosh.

My first feeling was one of relief that Ralph had decided to dispense with the karate. Our reputation couldn't stand him with another black eye and sore balls again. As it was, the situation was rapidly turning into farce.

I told Ralph that you could make a useful little tool by

putting a large stone or chunk of metal inside a couple of socks. It was the same principle as the PP9 cosh he had used, but with a denser payload.

Ralph could keep the socks and the object separate until the last moment. The object could be comparatively small, too, provided that it was hard and dense. The centrifugal force of the sock whipping around would give it maximum impact. Ralph liked the idea and asked me to get him a lump of metal from the tin shop.

At break-time that morning, I wandered away from where we usually sat for tea and slipped into the stores. This was where all the various metal-working tools were kept. I couldn't take any of those, though, because they were all on shadow boards. If one went missing, it would leave a very obvious gap.

At the back of the store I found an old tin box full of bolts, screws and washers. Nothing seemed large enough to interest me though. I rummaged through the box and suddenly found a golden-bronze coloured lump of metal, shaped like an extra large hen's egg. One end was drawn out, making it look like a large, golden teardrop.

At first I dismissed it because it was too small. When I picked it up, though, I couldn't believe how heavy it was. I didn't know from what type of metal it was made, but it was at least twice as heavy as I had expected.

I decided that it would do. I put it in my pocket and walked out into the shop. I went over to a window that had a small hole in its security grille. I dropped it through into some long grass, to be collected later.

That dinner-time, as everyone was returning from work, Barry and I went on to 'A' wing and up to Ralph's cell. He was sitting in a chair, reading.

'I've got it for you, Ralph,' I said. 'Have you got a couple of woolly socks?'

Ralph searched in a box under his bed and pulled out a pair

of grey, woollen, prison-issue socks. Putting one inside the other, I dropped the golden egg in and handed it to Ralph.

He swung it backwards and forwards experimentally. The frown on his face was still registering following his initial surprise at the smallness of the 'egg'.

Suddenly he swung it viciously against the wall. There was a loud, concussive 'bang', and a deep crack appeared right across the brick. It had, quite literally, cracked in half.

Ralph's frown was instantly replaced by one of consternation. He didn't say as much, but you could tell by his expression that he felt it was too dangerous. He only wanted to hurt Jackson, not kill him. Of course the trouble was that any blow with the 'egg' was liable to cause serious damage. I had a feeling that Ralph wouldn't use it.

Now the pressure was on Ralph to make his move. He had a bit of breathing space, though, because Jackson was still being minded by the screws.

A week dragged into two. Jackson started to get bolder, wandering further and further from his minders. We had known that they couldn't shadow him indefinitely. Ralph now had his chance. All that remained was for him to take it. But he still hesitated and dithered.

Suddenly, early one morning, Jackson disappeared. He was bound for the Midlands and some accumulated visits. Having had no visits for several months he was entitled to be transferred to his local prison, where his family could visit him more easily. He wouldn't be back for at least a month.

In some ways it was a satisfactory conclusion. It was beginning to look like Ralph would never make his move. And if he did, there was always the danger that he would badly hurt Jackson and get nicked for it. I would have backed Ralph to the hilt, but perhaps he had been a bit premature in doing Jackson merely on Jay's say-so in the first place. I was glad to see Jackson go.

He would be back in a month or so. Then Ralph would have

to decide what he was going to do all over again. But a month was a long time in Parkhurst. In between, literally anything could happen.

A few months later, following a sit-down protest on the compound, I and most of our group were shanghaied. Ralph remained though. Jackson duly came back from his visits. Ralph challenged him to another straightener. He lost again.

8. Nut-Nut

TERRY HILLMAN HAD all the criminal credentials to be one of our crowd; an experienced South London robber, he was doing 15 years for a big payroll robbery. He was staunch enough; there had never been any suggestion that he was a grass. At times he could be a right rebel. He certainly didn't have a good prison record. But a particularly contrary nature set him apart.

He was a burly, powerful fella, balding, with short, curly black hair. He had an aggressive way with him and regularly got into fights. He never went to the gym, so he was out of condition. However, he was a bit of a nutter and would lay into an enemy with whatever came to hand.

One of his problems was that, when in one of his awkward moods, he could fall out with friend and foe alike. Because of his volatile personality I used to called him 'Nut-Nut'. It was a private joke between us. Terry quite liked the image of being a bit crazy and dangerous.

Of all our crowd, I was the only one who got on with him at all. We had been in a tear-up together at the Scrubs. Having fought side by side, there was a bond of sorts. We weren't close pals, but I was one of his few defenders.

And he needed some defending. At Parkhurst he had got far too friendly with the screws. He wasn't a groveller or a yes-man by any means. He had a rough, familiar way with everyone, and if any screw had ever got saucy with him, Terry would soon have given him a volley.

He was the 'number one' on the hot-plate. This meant that,

amongst other things, he was in charge of the screws' tea-room. Part of his duties was to brew up for the screws, a job that the vast majority of cons at Parkhurst wouldn't have done. Apart from the fact that the screws were hated and no con would want to make tea for them, it was also seen as quite demeaning to be a screws' tea-boy.

This didn't faze Terry though. In fact he regularly compounded the felony by making them sandwiches from meal-time leftovers too. He got a few perks in return, but it hardly endeared him to the fellas.

Generally he wasn't liked. He wasn't publicly insulted, but a lot of people wouldn't speak to him. It didn't worry him, though, because he just surrounded himself with a small group of syco-phants. They were mostly weak low-lifes, whom Terry bullied. It was a wonder they stood for it at times. But, like courtiers around a king, without Terry they were nothing.

There were a couple of young screws on the wing, and Terry got on particularly well with them. Under different circum-stances, they could have admired his rough rebelliousness. They had both recently left the army after serving in Northern Ireland. They hated the IRA with a passion.

There were about ten IRA men at Parkhurst, three on our wing. They kept very much to themselves and never gave anyone cause to fall out with them. They were polite and eminently trust-worthy. Their crimes apart, they were principled men. I never heard of any of them pulling strokes. In a world where we were surrounded by potential enemies, we had nothing to fear from the IRA.

Some of our crowd didn't like them. Understandably, they strongly disapproved of the IRA's habit of putting bombs in places where civilians could get hurt. Many of the 'chaps' were quite right wing in their politics. There were more than a few 'Little Englanders'. If a bomb had ever gone off in London injuring large numbers of ordinary people, then our local IRA would definitely have had a severe come-back from the Parkhurst Londoners.

My own personal feeling was that, as they weren't grasses or liberty-takers, they were no threat to me. Parkhurst was full of people who were a very real threat. I would reserve my enmity for them.

There was one particular IRA man who seemed to be the local leader. The one most senior in rank always assumed the role of Commanding Officer.

He was a tall, gangling fella, who lived on the landing above mine. He was quiet to the point of being withdrawn, mixing only with the other IRA fellas. If you hadn't known he was IRA, you would never have guessed. Our two ex-army screws hated him.

Whether they actually asked Terry to do something about him or whether Terry suggested it himself, never came out. What was obvious, though, was that they hatched up a plot between them.

I was lying on my bed one dinner-time, dozing lightly. Everyone was locked up, and most of the screws had gone off for dinner. The wing was very quiet. Over the years you couldn't help but get into the habit of taking a quick nap over the dinner-time bang-up. There was little else to do, and the large, stodgy dinner inevitably had a soporific effect.

From time to time I could hear laughter from the direction of the screws' tea-room. I guessed that Terry was sitting in there with whichever two screws were on the dinner-time watch. Another habit of his that antagonized many of the fellas.

Almost subconsciously, I was aware of boots going up the metal stairs just outside my door. It wasn't a loud clatter, just the scuffing of leather on steel and the odd squeak of stressed metal. It wasn't unusual. Perhaps someone upstairs had rung his bell and the screws were going up to see what he wanted.

Suddenly, I heard the explosive sound of a cell door opening quickly. Now that was unusual. When the screws were off at mealtimes prisoners weren't supposed to be unlocked.

It could be a special search or a shanghai, but I hadn't heard any extra screws come on to the wing. Whatever it was, it was something out of the ordinary. Something that couldn't wait until the rest of the screws came back from dinner.

If I had needed any further convincing, the sharp cry of pain confirmed that something was up. I jumped off my bed and ran to press my ear to the door.

The tall IRA man had been dozing on his bed too. Unlike me, he hadn't heard the sound of boots coming up the stairs. Or, if he had, he hadn't paid it any attention. He hadn't heard Terry and the two young screws as they crept along the landing towards his cell either.

The first thing he knew was when the door crashed open, and Terry ran in. He had the sleeve of a jumper pulled down over his face as a mask. As the IRA man rose off his bed. Terry slashed him across the cheek with a Stanley knife. That was the scream that had aroused me.

As he threw his arm up to protect his face, Terry hit him across the opposite side of his head with the wooden baton he was holding in his left hand. The IRA man fell to the floor, and Terry continued to beat him.

Pausing just to put in a last couple of kicks, Terry spun round and rushed out of the cell. One of the screws banged the door behind him and slid the bolt home. The whole episode had lasted barely 30 seconds.

For several days I couldn't find out what had happened. Terry and the two screws obviously weren't talking. If the IRA man went sick with his injuries, no one saw him, and he didn't tell the screws how he had got them. He must have told the rest of the IRA fellas, but they always kept things to themselves.

They never made any sort of come-back. Terry could be very dangerous, and any move against him would have had to be a serious one. Tools would have been used, and it could quite easily have ended up with someone being killed.

Then there was the fact that Terry was a Londoner. The IRA fellas knew that Londoners stuck together at Parkhurst.

They weren't to know that very few of the Londoners there liked Terry though.

Finally, Terry obviously had the help of the screws. Looking at it from the IRA's perspective, it wasn't surprising that it was let go.

After about a week our crowd discovered what had happened. If we had found out immediately, we would have been more incensed. As it was, several other things had occurred in the intervening period. We were still disgusted though. The screws were the enemy. We wouldn't accept help from them under any circumstances. And as for joining together with them to attack another con, that was completely out of order.

However, the crucial point was that it didn't involve any of our group. We could have picked up the cudgels on the IRA man's behalf on a general point of principle, but similar points of general principle were arising every day. Life in Parkhurst was an ongoing Greek tragedy. We couldn't, and wouldn't, come to the help of everybody.

The important thing was that our firm was strong. Because of that no one gave us a hard time. No one would come at us unless we did something serious to them first. There were far softer targets than us.

The moral was that the IRA man had suffered because he and his crowd were comparatively weak. And, in Parkhurst, weakness was the ultimate sin.

Terry is still free. Over the years he has been involved in numerous tear-ups in clubs and pubs. His unquiet spirit forever drags him into conflict. It's a wonder he hasn't been killed.

The IRA printed an account of the attack in their paper An Phoblact. *They mentioned Terry by name. It was said that they would take their revenge. As of yet, nothing has happened. Perhaps they have had to take their place in the queue of all Terry's other enemies.*

9. Mr Nice-guy

I F THERE WERE one message that was repeatedly driven home at Parkhurst, it was that safety lay with the group. Its corollary was that mixing with mugs inevitably got you into trouble.

Membership of our group did have its risks, but the benefits far outweighed the drawbacks. We were physically safer than most other people in the jail, and that wasn't to be undervalued.

There were no fools in our group. Therefore we wouldn't be drawn into some major trouble because of sheer stupidity. Admittedly, Barry could be unpredictable, to say the least. But on balance, his other attributes made him a valued member of the group.

Mick was the oldest of our crowd. At 38 and with an 18-year sentence in front of him, his future looked particularly bleak. He had been a member of the most prolific and successful firm of robbers in the history of London armed crime. The supergrass on the firm had been a childhood friend. This made it especially hard for Mick to accept.

He had an easygoing, likeable personality, but he didn't live nearly tight enough for Parkhurst. He was not only polite and chatty to many of the screws but also on friendly terms with several people outside our group. Quite a few of these were rated as complete mugs by the rest of us. Time and again we would ask

Mick why he was mixing with someone or other who had a reputation for being a right berk. Mick would just smile and say that he was only being sociable.

Mick regularly talked to Peter, a young lifer who worked in the tailor's shop with him. Peter was only 22 and thoroughly immature with it. Rumour had it that he was innocent and had taken the rap for someone else. Whatever the circumstances, he hadn't come to terms with his sentence at all and was forever doing stupid things.

He was short, plump and had an innocent-looking babyface. His fairish hair and blue eyes completed a picture that resembled an overgrown schoolboy.

He didn't win much respect over his friendship with Ron. The Twins lived in the Security Wing and rarely came into contact with cons from the main prison. Ron was well known for his homosexuality. On the occasions when he was escorted through the prison, he would show-out to various young fellas. The vast majority didn't welcome the attention. A few of the mugs, though, were pleased to be acknowledged by someone as notorious as he, even if it were only because Ron fancied fucking them.

Peter was one of the latter. A Northerner, he had only read about Ron and Reg in the papers. He was quite flattered that Ron should notice him. He joined the growing band of young fellas who went over to the church each Sunday to pass messages across the pews to Ron.

Peter's closest friend was another lifer called Don. He was in his early 20s and came from the West Country. He was short and squat, with an elaborate, well-greased Elvis hairstyle. The long sideburns and dense designer stubble were an attempt to appear heavy. He worked out on the weights and walked about with an exaggerated body-builder's strut.

This macho image, though, hardly squared with his homosexual activity at the back of the cinema. If anything, it made his posing seem all the more ridiculous. Our crowd had nothing but contempt for him and referred to him as 'Deep Throat'. Barry especially detested him and was forever looking for an excuse to knock him out.

We didn't openly ever take the piss out of him though. He couldn't have a fight, but he could be very dangerous. Only a year earlier he had got a seven on top of his life sentence for seriously stabbing another con.

Peter and Don had enough neuroses between them to fill a case-book. They could never come to terms with the fact that, in the macho world of Parkhurst, their poofery only brought them contempt. Therefore, they were always doing things to try to prove how tough they were. They were dangerous fools and were to be avoided.

They saw things that our group and others got away with and regularly tried to imitate them. It rarely came off though. If they tried to have a drink of hooch, for example, the 'A'-wing screws would walk right in on them and break it up. Something they would never have tried with our group. This just served to increase their sense of inferiority.

On this particular day Peter and Don had made some hooch. One young screw, with whom Peter used to joke about, had already told them to get rid of it. Because of the informal nature of his relationship with him, perhaps Peter didn't believe he meant it.

It was mid-evening and time for people to return from the 'stage' rooms and have an hour's association on the wings before banging up. For this period the cells on 'A' wing would be unlocked. Peter and Don had chosen this time to have their drink. With two Thermos flasks full of the hooch they walked along the landing towards Peter's cell.

Two screws were standing on the bridge, near to Peter's cell. One of them was the young screw. As Peter and Don crossed the bridge, the young screw stepped out in front of them.

At this precise moment the gate at the end of 'A' wing was opened for those returning from the 'stage' rooms. There must have been 50 of us, both 'A' wing and 'D' wing mixed.

The 'A'-wing fellas started to spread out and head up to their landings. The 'D'-wing bunch, with Mick, Barry and I in the lead, headed for the stairs that led down to the 'ones', on our way through to 'D' wing.

As we approached the top of the stairs we were on the same level as the bridge that spanned the 'twos'. We could clearly see the two screws standing there, barely 30 feet away, with Peter and Don approaching.

I knew instantly that something was wrong. The signs were almost subliminal, but the two screws seemed to be waiting to pounce, and Peter and Don seemed on edge. A sixth sense picked up on the intangible air of tension.

I was immediately on my guard, but just carried on walking, saying nothing. I wasn't unduly concerned, because neither Peter nor Don were friends of our crowd. And, anyway, in a few seconds we would be down the stairs, passing underneath the bridge as we headed along the 'ones' on our way through to 'D' wing.

Suddenly, Peter turned towards us. As he saw Mick he called out, 'Mick, have you got a minute?'

Mick smiled his usual 'nice fella' smile and immediately ducked out of the crowd. Straightening his glasses across his nose, he headed along the 'twos' towards the place where the landing met the bridge.

Now, I slowed right down. Barry had got it, too, and slowed with me. The crowd of about 20 were forced to shuffle along behind us.

Mick was half-way there when the young screw made a grab for the flask that Peter was carrying. Peter punched him in the face, and they started to struggle. At the same time the second screw pulled out his stick and went to hit Peter with it.

I had no time for either Peter or Don, but now the situation had changed. In Parkhurst, whenever there was a row between a con and a screw, any decent con would take sides against the screw. Even if this meant getting physically involved in a fight. Also, Mick was so close to the action, he looked like being involved too.

By now I had reached the top of the stairs. I stopped abruptly and spread my arms wide, grabbing the railing either side. This forced the crowd following me to come to a halt.

'Oi,' I shouted loudly, 'put that fucking stick away.'

The screw stopped in mid-swing. He looked round and saw the crowd of cons standing there. The tight, hostile faces glared at him. The young screw stopped struggling with Peter and stepped back. They both realized that a major incident was only seconds away, an incident in which they could only come off worst.

Taking their chance, Peter and Don brushed past the screws and ran into Peter's cell. There was a banging and scraping as they barricaded the door behind them.

The effect of all this on Mick had been traumatic. One minute he had been bowling along the landing on what he thought was a social call, the next he was in the middle of a punch-up with two screws.

The pleasant smile had disappeared from his face to be replaced by a look of consternation. Fussing nervously with his glasses as he looked over his shoulder, he rapidly backtracked along the landing.

Still looking over his shoulder, he pushed through the crowd. He ducked under my outstretched arms and skipped quickly down the stairs. He hurried along the 'ones' towards the door that led to 'D' wing, continuing to glance up nervously at the 'twos' and the screws standing outside Peter's closed door.

Now that the situation was over, I dropped my arms and descended the stairs at the head of the crowd. Barry was cursing next to me.

'That fucking Mick, wanting to be Mr Nice-guy all the time. Perhaps now he'll know not to mix with mugs,' he fumed.

Barry was right, of course. Peter had tried to involved Mick, hoping to deter the screws from grabbing the hooch. He had taken advantage of his friendship with him. He would never have tried that with either Barry or me, who didn't so much as speak to him.

We walked through into 'D' wing and entered Mick's cell. He was sitting on his bed, still white around the gills.

'I thought he was going to give me some books,' he said as we came in.

'How many times do you have to be told about having it with mugs?' shouted Barry angrily. The thought of getting involved in a tear-up with the screws on behalf of Peter and Don, both of whom he detested, had really wound him up. For a moment I thought he was going to punch Mick.

If we had thought that Mick had learned his lesson, we were soon disappointed. The following day he was back to normal. Cheerfully joking with the screws and calling a cheery good morning to all and sundry, he bustled about the landing.

Barry and I watched, but said nothing. Mick had gone down a lot in our estimation. It wasn't so much that he had ignored everything we had said. We just couldn't forget the way he had run off and left us after we had stood by him and his mate Peter.

The most basic tenet of our group was loyalty. Where Mick was concerned, though, it was beginning to look like a one-way process. As far as Barry and I were concerned, next time he'd be on his own.

10. The Poof Doctor

BY AND LARGE the cons at Parkhurst remained oblivious to any changes of staff. The arrival of a new governor might be remarked on, but such was the barrier between cons and screws that virtually no relationship of any kind grew between them.

The screws actively discouraged any familiarity and kept to themselves. Similarly, most of the cons utterly detested the screws and only spoke to them when they had to. In fact, any con who became too close to the screws would quickly get himself a bad name. Various sanctions would follow, ranging from social ostracism to outright assault.

Exercise time, after the dinner-time bang-up, was the first real chance of the day for the cons to get together. Breakfast was always a hurried affair. The wings were locked off until movement to work, so you couldn't get about the place. On the way to work you would see people from other landings and other wings, but there was little time to talk.

By dinner-time, though, whatever gossip there was had been discussed in the work shops. During exercise, this gossip was passed on, so that by the end of the period you could have a pretty good idea of what had happened in the jail over the past 24 hours.

One exercise time the talk was all about the new doctor. Although all the rest of Parkhurst's staff were permanent, various local GPs visited to hold morning surgery. You could never be sure which of the four or five it would be, but it didn't really matter anyway, because they would always be guided by the resident medical screws. Each doctor would have his own, personal idiosyncrasies, but all would try to ensure continuity and never rock the boat. That was until the new doctor arrived.

Each morning about 20 men would report sick. Mostly it was a waste of time, because they would be fobbed off with pills and medicines. If an operation were needed, then it would be done in Parkhurst hospital. First-class, outside surgeons would operate, but it was the level of after-care that worried most cons. It was hard enough dealing with the hospital screws when you were fully fit. So the idea of lying helpless and at their mercy didn't appeal to many people.

The men reporting sick would be let through several gates into a small area adjacent to 'C' wing. Here they would sit on long benches outside the visiting doctor's office. They would go in, one by one, to discuss their problems with him. Also present, would be the hospital PO and another medical screw.

This exercise time several fellas were going off about the new doctor who had been on that morning. He had cancelled the treatment of men who had been on particular drugs for years. He had also stopped the daily allowance of milk for several people who had managed to wangle a pint of milk a day because of some medical condition.

All this was bad enough in itself, but, to add insult to injury, the new doctor was outrageously gay. Not just effeminate, the fellas emphasized, but absolutely raving. And the mid-seventies at Parkhurst were hardly liberated times.

By tea-time the jail was in an uproar. All sorts of dangerous lunatics were making dire threats about what would happen if the new doctor stopped their medication. The mere thought of having to go through the day straight made them even more uptight than usual.

The screws, especially the medical screws, were seriously worried. They knew what they could expect when certain cons started to experience withdrawal symptoms that had previously been suppressed by drugs. They also knew that they would be in the frontline when these men joined the treatment queue and demanded their usual medication. Drugging had become official policy at Parkhurst, because it kept people quiet.

The cons in general were very angry. Anything that smacked of a crackdown was like a challenge to them. They were well aware that privileges in prison weren't given gratuitously. They were given to keep people quiet and, as such, had to be fought for. Sometimes they had to be defended. The fact that the clamp-down might just be a personal initiative on the part of a new doctor didn't come into it. They didn't draw any distinction between prison doctors and prison management. They were all the same to them.

The following morning about 90 of us reported sick. They brought us through to the waiting area in batches of 20. It was quite an effective way of registering a protest, because, instead of sick parade being finished in an hour, it would now take all morning. The screws would have lots of extra work to do, which would put them behind in their other duties. And, as an added bonus, we would get a whole morning off work.

I had gone sick out of solidarity with the others. I was rarely ill and had little use for the doctors. However, I also wanted to have a look at the man who had caused all the uproar. The descriptions had sounded so exaggerated that I just had to see for myself.

About half an hour had gone by. There had been a steady flow of men going in and out of the doctor's room. On several occasions there had been muffled screams and shouts. The door would open and the medical screws would gently push the protester out, still shouting abuse at the doctor.

One or two had tried to attack him physically. The screws

had got between them and gently edged them out of the room. This was all very unusual, if for no other reason than, in similar circumstances, the heavy mob would have dragged the offender off to the chokey.

At last my turn came. I wasn't on any medication, but I did have some cream for my psoriasis. My excuse would be to ask for more cream. My name was called, and I walked into the room.

The doctor was sitting behind a large desk. Standing either side of him were the two medical screws. They both had grins on their faces, an anatomical feat that I would have previously thought impossible. I was soon to see why.

The doctor was in his late 40s, slim and wearing a suit of pastel beige. It had wide lapels and was entirely too trendy for Parkhurst. He had a long, smooth face and medium-length blond hair that was well slicked down, but curling at each temple. 'Yes, Parker, and what's the matter with you?' he trilled.

Despite what I had already heard, the voice and mannerisms still came as a shock. He spoke in a high falsetto, with accompanying breathlessness. The hand, head and eye movements were all greatly exaggerated.

There were plenty of poofs in Parkhurst, and many of them affected effeminate ways, but none remotely approached the level of high camp of our new doctor. He was a real screaming queen, all high-pitched voice and feminine gestures.

Now, the two medical screws were laughing unrestrainedly. I stood there, thoroughly embarrassed. All thoughts of picking an argument had vanished. I just wanted to get out of the room as quickly as possible.

The doctor couldn't fail to notice the reaction his behaviour was provoking, but he made no acknowledgement of it. He just sat there looking at me, waiting for an answer to his question.

I quickly explained about my psoriasis, secretly praying that he wouldn't ask to see it. I had a patch of the rash on my upper thigh, so it would have meant taking off my trousers. This would have provoked even greater merriment in the two screws. They already seemed to be greatly enjoying themselves.

The doctor listened, then wrote something down in a book in front of him.

'OK,' he said, 'I've renewed the Betnovate cream for another month.'

As he finished, I immediately turned and left the room.

I hadn't had any trouble with him, but there wasn't too much he could do with a request for such a simple treatment. Others, however, continued to be provoked. One got so incensed that he actually dived across the desk and grabbed hold of the doctor's lapels, before being bundled out.

The following day we heard that the new doctor wouldn't be coming again. It wasn't that his manner had been incompatible with that of a Parkhurst official. There were plenty of others whose manner was hostile, punitive and actively offensive, yet they continued to serve. It was the fact that he had ignored the medical screws' advice and gone against the unofficial policy of prescribing drugs for cons, just to keep them quiet. In his own way the new doctor had been as rebellious against the system as many of us cons.

11. Somebody Loves a Fairy at 40

ALTHOUGH THE NEW doctor's homosexuality compounded the insult of his attitude in the eyes of many cons, Parkhurst wasn't a hotbed of rampant homophobia. There was a fair degree of live and let live. Hypocrisy apart, the attitude of many of the 'chaps' was that if the poofs didn't bother them, they wouldn't bother the poofs.

There was always the problem of definition. It was generally agreed that anyone who took it up the bum was obviously a poof. However, quite a few people, at one time or another, in one jail or another, had had their cocks sucked. Did this make them poofs?

Most of them certainly didn't think so. Especially as they were either married or strictly heterosexual when outside.

I personally didn't think the issue very important. It was a subject of some embarrassment to me, but, when asked privately, I would offer the opinion that there were many ways to judge a man and his sexuality wasn't the most important. However, in public, I sometimes echoed the generally homophobic statements of the majority of the 'chaps'.

We were all aware that, as a term of abuse, the word 'poof' didn't have particularly negative or unmanly connotations. There were some poofs at Parkhurst who scored high on all the other manly, non-sexual indicators. Some were very dangerous with a blade. Some could have a right row. Others were very strong on the weights and had good physiques. Many were very staunch and never pulled strokes or grassed. Quite a few were well respected (nobody ever called Ronnie Kray a poof).

Often, when Barry was in a particularly homophobic state of mind, I would take the opportunity to remind him of some of the poofs I had met who were proud, honourable men. One day, just as he was raging about the 'poof doctor', I told him about Micky Blake.

At 42 Micky Blake was getting a bit too old to be a poof. Admittedly, he still had the slender figure of his youth. And his shoulder-length brown hair was still thick and strong, although shot through with grey in places. But his face!

There's an old saying in jail, 'It doesn't show on your shoes.' If it had, then Mick's would have been battered and nearly worn out. As it was, it was his face that had borne the brunt of the stress and strain.

What, in his youth, had been a pleasant, almost handsome, if slightly effeminate visage, was now deeply lined and worn. Time, that cruellest of satirists, had taken each and every part of the young face that had looked out on the world, and etched age and despair everywhere.

His once smooth forehead was now deeply rutted with lines that made for a perpetual frown. His eyes had sunk deep into a morass of crow's feet until now it seemed as if they peered out from deep pits.

The skin was stretched drum-tight, highlighting bony cheeks and jaw, almost as if the skull beneath was trying to force its way through. Its texture was waxy and lifeless, gone was the bloom of youth.

Perhaps the saddest feature was his mouth. The loss of all his teeth had caused it to sink inwards, puckering around his lips. He was very conscious of this and would try to shield his mouth with his hands when he spoke. No one, even early morning visitors to his cell, had ever glimpsed his false teeth.

The once elegant neck was as scraggy as a chicken's, with lined flesh hanging in folds. His Adam's apple, always prominent, protruded almost as starkly as his nose.

It was the face of someone who had been under the most intense pressure. Almost as if the wind had changed, fairytale-like, and a silent scream had been frozen there for ever.

Mick still tried to carry himself like a woman though. He would tilt his head to one side in a coquettish pose. Long, bony fingers would raise a cigarette to his lips in a manner that might have been temptatious a decade earlier. He would swing his hips as he swished on to the exercise yard.

Tragically, it all served to emphasize the cruel caricature of a middle-aged man trying to act like an attractive woman. Whatever had been, was gone, and would never be again.

Mick wasn't ideally suited for prison life. No thief or villain, he was basically a straight goer. A disastrous affair with a lover, who had used and abused him, then tossed him aside, had shattered his life. He had killed the fella out of sheer desperation, thinking no further than the act. Not caring what happened next, just so long as the terrible emotional trauma was ended.

The subsequent trial and life sentence had torn the heart out of him. He had plumbed such depths of grief and despair that only his basic life force had kept him going.

In many ways he was already dead. Prison was such a cold, emotionless existence that the pain often seemed to outweigh the pleasure. He had had affairs, but they had all been shallow and unsatisfactory. He had searched for love; his partners for lust.

Now, eight years into his life sentence, the future looked bleak. He still had several years to serve, and then what? The incessant pressure had eaten away at him, eroding the very youth from his body. His sensitive, caring nature was totally at odds with the uncouth, violent people around him. Despite his crime he wasn't a violent person himself. This put him at all sorts of disadvantages in the prison milieu. He spent whole days looking for just a moment's solace.

Luckily, Long Lartin was a liberal prison. A laid-back regime allowed a varied subculture to flourish. There was a wide-spread gay scene that was more overt than in many jails. Some of the 'chaps' dabbled, some didn't. It was no big deal. No one was ostracized over it. There was all the usual hypocrisy, but nobody was ever bashed just for being a poof.

Having said that, the 'chaps' would never have 'fem' poofs in the company. Those that had their own, regular poof would live with them in the domestic situation. But out on exercise, in the gym, out on the sportsfield, the 'chaps' would congregate and talk of crime, violence and other macho things. The poofs would congregate on their own. A mirror image of the clubs outside, where the 'chaps' would stand in a crowd at the bar and their women in a group in the corner.

Mick, though, wasn't one of the 'chaps'. He was no thief or villain and had no hard reputation. For him, there was a subculture of poofs who kept to their own company. They weren't dominant or influential in any way. They weren't even a unified group. Regularly, they were harried and harassed by more violent cons.

A group of them generally gathered out on the exercise yard, up against 'E' wing where the path met the main yard. Eight or nine, mostly young fellas, would stand gossiping and smoking. All were openly gay.

The talk would be of boyfriends and general prison gossip. But mostly it would be of boyfriends. In many ways Mick was the senior queen. He was certainly the oldest, but he had also served longer in prison.

He was a Londoner and had a reputation for being staunch. There had never been any suggestion that Mick would ever grass anyone. He stood up to the screws too. He had a quick, vicious tongue. Many was the screw who had backed off under a tirade of abuse and innuendo. Mick didn't pull strokes either.

Because of these qualities most of the London 'chaps' accepted him. There was nothing in it. His sexuality went unmentioned. Mick wasn't screamingly camp anyway, so there was no embarrassment. There was a degree of mutual respect.

Amongst the 'fem' poofs Mick was virtually unique in this. He had no great 'in' with the 'chaps' though. However, as they totally blanked nearly all the other fem poofs, it was significant. It gave him a certain standing.

Unfortunately it was virtually all he had. Most of the other poofs were quite young. They regularly talked about their various affairs; Mick could only talk. Usually he was on his own. Behind his back he was regarded as something of a pathetic figure.

Recently he had had a fling with Aaron, an uncouth lout of a fella in his late 30s, who was doing life for manslaughter. A country fella through and through, he was no professional criminal. He weighed a strapping 15 stone. With a big bushy beard on an enormous head he could have been a biker. He certainly looked the part and had the attitude.

Aaron, better than anyone, realized that the killing had been a pure blunder. The 'chaps' regarded him as a complete berk, although probably a bit of a handful in a punch-up. But he was a big, strong fella, possessed of a craziness and a desperation born of his life sentence. If his crime didn't make him the part, then he would act the part to establish his reputation. Aaron was one of the most disruptive prisoners in the jail.

Loud and always arguing with the screws, Aaron was a perpetual bully, who tormented those weaker than himself. He had a habit of playfully punching people, until their arm was bruised and swollen. That it was playfully malicious rather than purely wicked didn't come into it. He made many a young fella's life a misery.

Aaron hadn't been into poofs before he came into prison. His appetites, though, were as uncouth as his manners. In the absence of women he had to find some way to slake his desires. In his own inimitable way, he took rather than asked.

It wasn't a courtship with Mick. They just happened to be on the same wing, and Aaron pushed himself on to him. At first, it was merely a knockabout friendship. Aaron would walk into his cell and joke and play about.

Perhaps Mick was flattered by the attention. Perhaps the loneliness had grown intolerable. Anyway, Mick encouraged him. Soon he was one of Aaron's possessions.

Once whatever novelty there had been in the relationship had worn off, Aaron treated Mick exactly the same as others in his circle. Because Mick spent more time around him, though, he took the brunt of it. Soon his life was a nightmare. He was constantly at the centre of Aaron's oafish behaviour and brutish desires.

To complain brought playful punches that hurt and bruised. Their sex life was chaotic. Aaron would burst in and take him when he felt like it. Sometimes he would just throw Mick to the floor and fuck him with the cell door wide open. It was hardly a romance.

There was no escape for Mick. No one cared enough for him to intercede. To go to the screws would have labelled him a grass. At his wits' end he demanded a move to another wing. The screws knew what had been going on. Within a day Mick had moved from 'A' wing to 'E' wing. He would still bump into Aaron about the prison, but they would only meet in passing. He had escaped.

This had all been several weeks earlier. The recent memory was still painful to Mick. For a while he had been pleased to be on his own. When he stood with the other poofs out on exercise and listened to the trials and tribulations of their lives with their boyfriends, he was glad to be out of it.

The feeling didn't last though. Long hours sitting alone in his cell or in the TV room soon brought back the old familiar emptiness. Loneliness permeated his soul like a bitter winter. It was barely preferable to life with Aaron.

Mick's recent troubles had been no great drama played out on a public stage. The vast majority of cons didn't even know who he was and had remained oblivious to the whole affair. Those who did know had their own lives to lead. If they sympathized, their own situations took all of their energies. They noticed the sad and lonely figure as he went about the jail, but quickly forgot as soon as he passed.

The weather had been brightening up for a while now. Evenings had grown light and the cold bite of winter was gone from the air. Evening association started, and the fellas were allowed out on the sportsfield for a couple of hours each evening.

People who hadn't seen much of each other through the winter months renewed old acquaintances. Impromptu games of five-a-side football proliferated on the Redgra pitch, often with twice that number on each side. Runners strode out around the perimeter of the great field. Men stood in groups talking. Smaller groups walked up and down.

People who had been confined to the incestuous, cloying social circle of their own particular wing through the dark months, now had the opportunity to make new friendships or extend old ones. In the dead world of Long Lartin it was a brief period of rebirth.

One evening Mick was seen talking to a dark-haired young fella close to the Redgra pitch. For those who knew about the recent past and had been used to seeing Mick on his own, it was a significant, if minor, event. When they were seen together the next evening, walking around the field, there were knowing looks and the odd remark. Still, it was no big deal. Neither was a well-known 'face', with either power of influence. It was hardly the talk of the nick.

As the weeks went by, the pair became inseparable. Whether on the sportsfield, in the pay queue or in the cinema, there was Mick and the dark-haired young fella. They took to lingering in the corridors together. They could be seen waiting outside each other's wings. People were convinced that Mick had finally found himself a young fella.

In many ways it was a strange match. Bob P. was a Scouse fella in his mid-20s, who lived on the same landing as I did. He was quiet and unassuming. He hung around with a couple of other young fellas and generally kept a low profile. If you noticed him at all, you could be forgiven for wondering what he was in prison for. He didn't seem particularly criminal.

We always spoke in passing, but I was caught up in running a poker table, collecting on our football coupon and generally ducking and diving. Our crowd were all 'A' men and quite no-torious. Life was demanding and hectic, as life can only be for someone who aspires to be a 'face' in prison.

It if hadn't been for the fact that Bob was also on the 'A' list, I probably wouldn't have noticed him at all. As it was, I knew he was doing life for killing his girlfriend. In the violent world of Long Lartin he was very much a lightweight.

Long Lartin was a modern prison involving much state-of-the-art technology. The wings were laid out like campus accommodation, with a central enclosed stair-well running up to the landings.

Each landing was a complete floor, with two corridors of cells either side. Each corridor was quite wide and well lit, although the ceilings were low. At the end was a full-length, barred window, through which daylight poured. There were eight cells either side of each corridor.

Bob's was the sixth cell along on the left, two past mine.

Consequently, I often bumped into him on the landing or saw him go past as I sat in my cell. Occasionally he and his mates would have a bet on our football coupon. That was virtually the only real contact I had with him.

As far as I knew, he wasn't into poofs at all. He had never been seen with any of the more infamous ravers, and his name had never been mentioned in any of the regular scandals that blew up.

The first thing I knew of the liaison was when Micky Blake began to appear regularly on our landing. I knew Mick by sight but had rarely had reason to speak to him. I knew, of course, that he was a notorious poof and that he lived on 'E' wing.

It wasn't nosiness. There were good, practical reasons for being aware of who came on to your landing. Your cell was a place where you relaxed and your guard could be down. It was an ideal place for an enemy to attack you.

Mick was no threat to anybody though. I noted his constant comings and goings, found out the reason, then thought no more about it. It was none of my business. However, I did wonder what a young fella like Bob was doing with a raddled old queen like Mick. Perhaps he had never recovered from the rejection by his girlfriend.

Now Mick was in his element. His life had a whole new meaning again. He would hurry from his wing or from his work shop to meet Bob. Then they would stroll about, enjoying each other's company.

It had caused quite a stir amongst the crowd of poofs who regularly met on the exercise yard each day. Mick now had a young, well-mannered fella, who hadn't done the rounds amongst them. He obviously thought quite a lot of Mick and treated him well. Reflecting on some of their own, low-life boyfriends, they wouldn't have minded someone like Bob themselves.

The only negative aspect of the relationship for Mick was that they lived on different wings. For long periods each day they would be apart, both sitting alone in their respective cells waiting for the wing doors to open so they could be together again.

Although to go on another wing wasn't strictly allowed, sometimes Mick would slip upstairs on to Bob's landing. This was when I would see him hurry past my door. It wasn't very satisfactory though. They could only have a few minutes together, and if an unsympathetic screw was on the wing door he wouldn't allow Mick in at all.

Mick decided to try to get a move on to Bob's wing. Other people had changed wings, in fact he had done it himself only three months earlier. He duly made the application and went before the Governor.

The screws knew the real reason behind the move though. They had noticed the comings and goings. They didn't openly encourage such things, but others had got a move for similar reasons. However, Bob was still very young. Perhaps they felt that he should be protected from Mick's corrupting influence. The move was refused.

They still met around the prison. Mick slipped up to Bob's cell on occasions, but the affair had now an air of tragedy about it. Mick complained long and loud to all who would listen about the unfairness of being refused a move. Theirs had become a public and ongoing saga in the life of the institution.

Late one Tuesday afternoon shortly before tea-time lock-up, I was sitting in my cell with the door open, eating my meal. Suddenly, there was a shout from the direction of the stairs and the sound of running feet. As I looked up, I saw Mick run past my door. I carried on eating.

Seconds later, there was the tramp of heavy feet as two screws hurried past. I was on my feet instantly. If it was trouble, then it affected me. Friends of mine on the landing could be involved. I came out of my cell and looked along the landing.

The two screws had stopped outside Bob's cell. One of them had his mouth up against the crack of the closed door. 'Don't be silly now,' he shouted. 'Come on out, and you won't be nicked.'

There was no reply. Twice more he shouted out the same command. Still there was no answer. He turned the handle and pushed at the door. It wouldn't budge. He turned to the other screw, and they had a whispered conversation.

Chris, a pal of mine who lived opposite, was already out on the landing. Catching his eyes I mouthed, 'What's up?'

'Mick's barricaded up with Bob in his cell,' he mouthed back.

The cells were about seven feet long, six inches longer than the length of the bed. If you pulled your bed out across the door and wedged something in the narrow gap, you could effectively barricade your door. All the pushing in the world wouldn't get it open.

There was a method. It involved fetching a long, heavy jack and prising the door off. The process would take several minutes and did considerable damage. The door and door lining would be smashed and the opposite wall damaged.

Further, it rated as a serious incident and could raise the temperature of the jail. There was always the danger that those inside would fight back. Then rumours of brutality could start, triggering off a major revolt. The screws tried to talk people out first.

It was close to the five o'clock lock-up now though. Neither Bob nor Mick could go anywhere. Perhaps they just wanted to be together for the hour and would come out again when the wing unlocked again at six. The screws left them and walked to the end of the corridor.

I went into my cell and shut my door. Within seconds, I heard the clicks as the computerized locking system locked each door. A screw came along, tried each door handle and looked through the observation flap to check that everyone was inside their cells.

I heard him stop about where Bob's cell was. He rattled the handle then shouted out, 'Are you in there?' There was no reply. I guessed that Bob had covered his observation flap up from the inside.

Six o'clock came, and the sound of clicking ran around the landing again as the doors unlocked automatically. As I came out of my cell, I saw a screw at Bob's door turning the handle. The door wouldn't open, though, so Bob and Mick must still have been barricaded in.

There were knowing looks and some laughter amongst the rest of the fellas, but it was nothing to do with anyone else. The screw walked away from Bob's door, and everyone else went about their business.

During the evening I happened to see the Chief walk by my door. This was quite unusual as he rarely came up on the landings. As Chiefs went, he wasn't a bad fella. He had had all the hard times when he was a young screw down the Moor. Now, in the twilight of his career, he just wanted a quiet life.

Most of the 'chaps' got on with him well enough and called him Percy. He knew where the power lay amongst the cons and went out of his way to get on with the 'faces'. Sometimes it gave the ordinary screws the hump. Often, he would walk on to a wing and go to the cells of the 'faces', totally ignoring the screws.

It was good psychology. You always knew that if you had a problem, rather than having a tear-up, you could go to Percy, and he would work something out. Some screws called it appeasement. Percy called it good management. He certainly averted a lot of trouble at Long Lartin.

At times he admitted that he quite liked the 'chaps'. He would rather deal with them because at least he knew where he stood. Both shared the outlook of the old school.

I had to smile to myself when I saw him going along to Bob's cell. This wasn't the sort of problem he liked to deal with. No doubt he felt it was all quite embarrassing. You could negotiate with a couple of the 'chaps' who probably wanted some straight-forward concession. What did you say to two ravers who just wanted to rump each other?

Nine o'clock came around and evening lock-up. As we returned to our cells, Percy was still at Bob's door. It didn't seem like they were coming out. The electronic locking went on, keeping us behind our doors for the night. There was no sound along the landing outside Bob's door, they were being left together until the morning.

We unlocked for breakfast the following day, and they were still barricaded in. No doubt Bob had stocked up on food and water, but, even so, his two young mates from the cell above had lowered some down.

I secretly wondered what they had done about slopping out. They had no toilet, and it wasn't the done thing at Long Lartin to throw it out of the window. I was sure it must be getting a bit fetid in there. Perhaps true love was sharing the same piss-pot!

The work-bell went, and the wing emptied as the fellas went off to the work shops. Chris and I were wing cleaners, so we started on our daily duties. At about ten o'clock we returned to my cell for our usual cup of coffee.

As we sat there we saw Percy go by, heading for Bob's cell again. There was a muffled conversation, which gradually grew louder. Then he hurried past again, head down, with an angry look on his face.

He must have spun around, because, suddenly, he was standing in my doorway. 'Look, Norman,' he said, addressing me with no preliminaries, 'I've been as fair as I can with them. I've let them stay in there together all night, even though P——'s an 'A' man and should only be locked up on his own. I had to report it to the Home Office. It's rapidly making me a laughing stock. Now, if they're not out by eleven I've been ordered to jack the door off and drag them out.'

Percy paused, clearly embarrassed by the way he had

blurted it all out. Chris and I looked at each other. If either of us had so much as smiled, we would both have burst out laughing. Percy was really in a dilemma. He couldn't leave them indefinitely. Yet if he jacked the door off, it could lead to an incident that might spark off the jail.

'Can't you talk to them for me, Norman?' he asked. 'Find out what they want. If I can make any reasonable concession, I will.'

He had just tried to put me right in the middle. Reasonable fella or not, there was no way I was going to do a screw's job for him. It could very easily be misconstrued. That was how you could get yourself a bad name.

However, it wasn't unknown for other cons to act as a go-between to resolve a situation to the mutual satisfaction of both sides. There were several factors involved though. I would have to think about it.

'Give me a couple of minutes to think about it, Percy,' I said. 'I'll come down to the office and find you.' Percy nodded his head and walked off.

As soon as he went, I turned to Chris. 'You know what's going to happen don't you? At eleven o'clock the screws will come around and try to lock up all the cleaners. They won't want us about when they jack the door off. We'll have to tell them to fuck off, in solidarity with Bob and Mick. There will be a tear-up, and we'll be dragged away down the block. Then they'll jack the door off, and Bob and Mick will come out like lambs. They certainly won't have a tear-up.'

Chris nodded in agreement. 'Those pair of clowns won't have a fight, that's for sure,' he said. The seriousness of the situation had just dawned on him.

I stood up and walked along to Bob's door. Knocking loudly I shouted, 'Bob, Mick, this is Norman. Listen 'cause I want to talk to you.'

There was the sound of movement inside, then whatever

was blocking the observation flap was removed. I looked through and instantly regretted it.

There, barely a yard away, was Mick. Twenty-four hours without shaving hadn't improved his looks. He stood in one of his classic poses, cigarette in one hand with the wrist bent, other hand on his hip, with his head tilted to one side. But, horror of horrors, he didn't have his teeth in. The puckered hole where his mouth was looked like someone had just thrown a brick through it.

Bob stood behind and to one side of him. His young face seemed pale and he had an embarrassed, hang-dog look about him. He couldn't meet my eyes. I could understand his embarrassment.

Still, that wasn't my concern. People did strange things in prison. We were all under the greatest of pressure. My loyalty wasn't to them as individuals. It was to two fellow cons in trouble.

'Right,' I shouted. 'When they jack the door off at eleven o'clock, are you going to fight them?'

Mick shook his head. 'What about you, Bob?' I queried. He shook his head too. 'Well, in that case, as you're coming out anyway, you might as well negotiate for some concession now whilst you're in a position of strength, hadn't you?' They both nodded in unison.

'But can we trust what they say?' asked Mick worriedly.

'Well, I'm involved now,' I said. 'If Percy goes back on his word I'll do so much damage that he'll wish he had just jacked the door off in the first place. And he knows I'll do it too. So that's the only guarantee you've got.'

'OK,' said Mick. There was a pause.

'Well, what do you want?' I asked.

He thought for a minute and turned to Bob. Bob hadn't said a word. It was easy to see who made all the decisions. I could safely bet that this hadn't been Bob's idea at all.

Turning back towards me, Mick suddenly came to a decision. 'We know that we'll have to go down the block for a while. We don't mind that so long as they don't shanghai either of us out afterwards,' he said.

'You're sure now?' I queried. They both nodded their heads. 'Right, I'll go down and tell Percy. You two had better get some things together.'

Chris had been standing close by. He had heard most of what had been said. 'They're coming out,' I told him as I walked past.

I went downstairs to the wing office. The Chief was standing inside, talking to several screws. He looked up and saw me. He stepped outside and motioned me into an empty office nearby.

'Well, I've spoken to them, Percy,' I said, 'and they'll come out provided that you guarantee that neither of them will be shanghaied out of the jail.'

'They've got that,' he said immediately. 'You've got my word.'

'The only trouble is,' I continued, 'that I'm involved now. If anything happens, and they are shanghaied, it will make me look very bad. Then I will have to do something personally.'

Percy recognized the implied threat. He knew of the many violent incidents I had been involved in during the recent past. 'Norman,' he said, 'I give you my word.'

'OK, Percy, let them have a few minutes, and they will be down.'

I went back upstairs and along to Bob's door. I knocked and looked through the flap. Mick and Bob both turned to look at me.

'It's me again,' I shouted. 'I've spoken to the Chief, and he swears to me that you won't be shanghaied. He's waiting downstairs.' With that, I turned around and went back into my cell.

Chris followed me in. We sat down to finish our coffee, which was now barely warm. About a minute went by and I heard Bob's door open. It closed again; there was the sound of feet shuffling, and Mick and Bob appeared in my doorway. Each held a carrier-bag.

'Thanks for your help,' said Mick sheepishly. Mercifully, he had his teeth in now. 'Yes, thanks,' said Bob from behind him. I waved my hand and nodded my head as if to say, 'OK, don't mention it.' They turned and carried on along the landing.

The following day I heard that they had been given 14 days in the chokey. It was a bit steep, seven would have done. But I guessed that Percy was getting his revenge.

Over the next fortnight I largely forgot about the incident. I wasn't one to worry about anything, but I was aware that it wouldn't be over for me until they were both back on their respective wings again.

I didn't count the days, but eventually someone told me that they were both up. I hadn't seen them myself yet, but no doubt they were off somewhere together commiserating with each other after the loneliness of solitary. Later I saw Bob up on the landing. Percy had kept his word.

Once again the two lovers were to be seen together all over the jail. Out on the sportsfield, in the pay queue, at the cinema and on the yard, the two of them, inseparable as always, huddled up together deep in conversation. They had failed in their attempt to be together all the time, but what they had was better than being apart for ever.

12. Hitler's Child

EVERY WORKING–CLASS area, every generation, throws up a young hard-nut, a youth, mature before his time, who is as tough and game as men years his senior. In the early Sixties, Jackie Clark filled this role in London's Notting Hill.

At 19 he was a strapping 13 stone, with a big, barrel chest, powerful shoulders and a craggy, dark-shaven jaw. His broken, hooklike nose disbarred him from any claims to handsomeness. With his thick shock of jet-black hair, it even made him look a bit sinister. But he had narrow hips, was very light on his feet, and his jaunty air gave him a devil-may-care attitude.

Jackie could have a right row. He had become the 'daddy' of every borstal he had ever been in, and he had been in most of the tough ones. He had been good at boxing and might have gone far if he'd had the discipline. Even so, with his brawny physique, it gave him a decided edge over most people.

He was a thief and invariably ran with an older crowd than his contemporaries. It didn't really surprise anyone when he finally got four years for a tie-up and went into 'A' wing at the Scrubs. In those days 'A' wing was the boys' wing, where young prisoners under 21, or YPs, were held. All were doing fixed sentences rather than borstal. By YP standards four was a long sentence. A three was counted as severe and usually came as retribution for several Post Office robberies or scores of serious burglaries.

Jackie arrived just after I did. I was doing six years for shooting my girlfriend. I had originally been charged with capital murder, but the fact that she had a gun too saved me. The manslaughter verdict and heavy sentence made me instantly notorious on 'A' wing. I didn't think that I was particularly tough; there were plenty on 'A' wing who could have done me in a punch-up. But everyone seemed to treat me with a certain deference. I didn't know what they could see that I couldn't, but as it made life a lot easier for me, I played the role out for what it was worth.

I knew Jackie from outside. I had been in his company a few times, although I usually went about with his younger brother. Also, Jackie had been out with my sister. This didn't make him a member of any particularly exclusive club, though, because many of the local 'chaps' had taken her out. Ann was a stunningly beautiful and intelligent, blonde girl of 15. She was sophisticated beyond her years. It didn't last long with Jackie, probably more her fault than his.

This gave me a kind of bond with Jackie. We were both off the same manor, but dozens of others in 'A' wing were from Notting Hill too. The main thing we had in common, though, was that, as our four and six were classed as long-term sentences, we would both be going to Wakefield, the centre for all YPs doing over four years. So we hung around together and got to know each other quite well. By the time we left for Wakefield we were good pals.

Tony Davey was as different from Jackie as different could be. At six feet three and only 17 years old, his skinny frame made him seem all arms and legs. His greased-back, black hair was unfashionably long. His youthful baby face was spoiled by a longish nose. Despite a certain brashness he was quite shy. This shyness, as much as his gangling frame, caused him to stoop as he walked.

Tony was very intelligent. He had passed several GCEs at school but seemed to resent these academic laurels as evidence of conformity. For he strongly fancied himself to be a rebel. He was quickly seduced by the simplistic appeal of Fascism and founded the Crawley branch of Union Movement, the organization behind Sir Oswald Moseley's British Fascist Party. It had small 'bookshops' or offices in a couple of the major cities. It was very much a fringe party, though, a bizarre collection of naive idealists high on faded dreams of empire.

The Crawley branch of Union Movement didn't have much of a grassroots following. In fact it had six members, all young acquaintances of Tony. He was in charge because he had founded the party. He wasn't a natural leader, though, and his immature silliness soon led to a leadership challenge.

George was a year younger than Tony. He was a small athletic youth with a lively personality. His saucy self-confidence made him the born leader of the group. Before long there was a palace coup.

It didn't make the local papers, but one day George and the other four told Tony not only that George was now the leader of the Crawley branch of Union Movement but that Tony was also barred from membership. He wasn't summoned before an improvised committee or anything. They just told him to piss off because he wasn't part of their gang any more.

Tony wasn't naturally aggressive, and his lanky build didn't lend itself to feats of physical prowess. However, he was fanatically proud. He had a deeply held code of honour and duty. The pain and embarrassment caused by public rejection, coupled with a sense of perceived inadequacy, combined to give him a murderous resolve. Quite calmly, coldly and logically, he decided to kill George. It wasn't a crime he expected to get away with, so there wasn't a lot of planning to do. There was a process, though, that had a chilling likeness to ritual.

Without telling anyone what he intended to do, Tony made his preparations. He drew all of his savings out of the Post Office. He spent two weeks drinking every night, lavishing money on a casual girlfriend. Just before all of it was gone, he went into the local sporting-goods shop and bought a hunting knife. It was similar to a Bowie knife and had an eight-inch-long blade.

Tony chose Saturday and Crawley High Street as the time and place of reckoning. There were scores of people about as he walked down the street in the bright sunshine, the big knife tucked in the back of his waistband, hidden by his jumper.

Up ahead he saw George, just as he had known he would. He was being carried along by the inevitability of the situation now. Everything was right. The sunlight bathed him in a golden hue. What finer setting could he have to carry out this honourable act of revenge than right here in his local high street?

A couple of weeks had passed. As far as George was concerned, much of the venom had gone out of the dispute. However, he was disturbed by the sight of a new, more confident Tony, carrying himself erect as he bore down on him. He seemed to have the beginnings of a smile curling at the corners of his mouth. It was a knowing smile, born of some secret knowledge. If it had been midnight instead of midday, then George would have been seriously concerned.

The encounter was pleasant enough. From Tony's manner it seemed like he had forgotten their falling out. His unusually confident mien, though, still made George uneasy. But no sooner had they met than it was over. A couple of sentences were exchanged, and Tony was past him.

George continued on, up the high street. He discounted his fears in such a public place, surrounded by so many people. Directly behind him, though Tony had spun around and pulled the knife from his waistband. Raising it double-handedly above his head, he plunged the long blade into George's back, the force of the blow causing George to stumble forwards. Tony tore the blade free, plunging George several more times before a final, climatic blow left the knife buried up to the hilt in his spine.

It all happened so quickly. Passers-by stood frozen in shock as the gory tableau played itself out. Leaving George on the pavement in an ever widening pool of blood, Tony walked casually down the high street, into the police station and gave himself up.

George took a whole day to die, longer than the subsequent trial. That wasn't much of a contest. Tony pleaded 'guilty' and was sentenced to Her Majesty's Pleasure, the juvenile equivalent of 'life'. It wasn't a particularly memorable murder, except for the local inhabitants of Crawley that is. There was one particularly chilling piece of evidence though. It was given by a young policewoman, a strapping country girl. She described how she had stood over George in the local hospital and pulled with all her strength to get the knife out of his back. Tony had meant it all right.

Immediately after the killing Tony had been lodged in the same 'murder charge' ward of Brixton Prison Hospital as me. Two things were very plain. The first was that he was quite resigned to being found guilty. The second that he didn't regret killing George one bit.

Tony and I were the only YPs on the ward, the others ranging in age from their early 20s to their late 60s. It was natural enough that we pal up together. It wasn't a close friendship, just two young fellas sharing a common situation.

It soon transpired that I had seen George before. My girlfriend's elder brothers, Phil and Jim, were bodyguards to Sir Oswald Moseley. I occasionally attended meetings with them. One evening, Moseley was speaking at West London's Kensington Town Hall. As the large room filled up Phil and Jim were doing their usual stewards' role, showing some to their seats but others the door through which they had just entered.

The hall was nearly full when two tall young fellas walked in. Both had long black hair, black leather jackets and tight jeans. To

Phil and Jim, long steeped in the thuggish arts but firm believers in proper dress for proper occasions, they looked like two yobbos. Not at all like smart young Fascists; more akin to the anarchist rabble who often tried to disrupt the meetings.

'What do you two girls want?' Phil asked, pleasantly enough, as he stepped in front of them.

'We're from the Crawley branch of Union Movement,' replied Tony, showing the membership card that had come through the post and that he so treasured.

Fellow Fascists were a bit thin on the ground at the best of times. And perhaps they would shape up when they got older. Anyway, they both had valid memberships. Phil showed them to their seats.

I was amazed when this came out in conversation with Tony. Two young fellas from different parts of the country, thrown together by most unusual circumstances. Yet we had met before. Early evidence of the smallness of the criminal world.

I was convicted and left for the Scrubs a couple of weeks before Tony. By the time he arrived I was firm friends with Jackie. Because of his particularly long sentence, Tony was put in a cell on the 'ones', close to the screws' office.

If Jackie's sentence, and my own, had attracted interest amongst the other YPs, then Tony's caused utter dismay. Before he had arrived, mine was the longest on the wing. Now there was a constant coming and going outside Tony's door, as young fellas peered through the spy-hole to have a look at the sort of fella who could murder someone and get HMP.

He was only at the Scrubs a few weeks before they moved him to Wakefield. He didn't do anything very unusual in that time, mostly stayed quietly in his cell. He did indulge in one small act of rebelliousness though.

The screws on 'A' wing were bullies to a man. They took

advantage of their relative size and maturity to dominate the YPs. They were on us every second we were unlocked, and often when we were behind our doors as well. We hated them with a passion. Anything done against them had our heartfelt support.

One of the main ways they would wind us up was over our mail. Strictly speaking you were only allowed to receive as many letters as you sent out. As we were only issued with two letters a week, there was always an imbalance between incoming and outgoing. For young fellas, many of whom were away from their families for the first time, mail was all important. It reminded them that they weren't forgotten and that someone still cared for them. Equally, many a parent would be thoroughly distraught at the thought of their son being locked up in prison. Their letters desperately sought reassurance that their boy was coping.

This didn't matter a damn to the screws. You would have thought that none of them had ever been a parent themselves. One of the censors was a pure pig. He stuck to the letter of the rule rigidly. He regularly sent back excess mail. In his infinite wisdom he would also decide whether a relationship was serious and proper. He had stopped several fellas writing to their girlfriends.

He was a morose, bad-tempered Welshman in his early 50s. Balding, with a fat face and even fatter gut, it was hard to imagine anyone caring for him. If he had ever come into prison he would never have received a single letter. Perhaps he realized this and that was what made him so hard where others' mail was concerned. We were convinced that if he had his way, we would get no mail at all.

Early each morning he could be seen in the censor's office on the 'ones' working through the stack of outgoing mail. He would quickly scan each letter, looking for swear-words or criticism of the prison. Offenders were sent for and their letters handed back with instructions to rewrite. The majority passed his inspection though. These he would moisten with a little rubber roller resting on a damp pad, then he would seal them.

It was a constantly recurring ritual. All outgoing mail had to be in by 8 a.m., before we went to the work shops. The censor always had the mail completed a couple of minutes before work-call. He would finish with an air of finality, putting the roller and pad in his desk drawer.

One morning Tony came in with his letter seconds before work-call and just after the censor had put away his stuff. Tony apologized for being late and explained that it was an important letter to his mother. With bad grace, the censor snatched it from Tony's hand and started to read it.

Tony left. He paused outside and looked through the crack in the mailbox to see whether the censor was going to put it in the pile of outgoing mail or leave it on the side for tomorrow.

The censor finished reading the letter. He didn't bother to get the roller and pad out of his drawer. He just licked the envelope, sealed it and threw it on the outgoing pile.

A couple of times a week Tony would deliberately wait until the last minute before hurrying in and handing over his letter. Technically he was still in time, but this didn't stop the censor from giving him a volley. Each time, Tony would go outside and peer through the crack to watch the censor seal his letter. Then he would walk away with a smile on his face.

One morning I saw the smile and asked him what he was so pleased about. He explained how the censor didn't bother to get the little roller out when he brought his letter in late, just licking the envelope to seal it. For the past couple of weeks Tony had been wiping his dick all over the sticky part of the envelope. Then he would rush in at the last moment and hand it to the censor. He would go outside and peer through the crack, just in time to see him lick it. It gave Tony a big thrill to be getting back at him. 'The censor's plating me by proxy,' he would say, laughing.

Jackie and I duly arrived at Wakefield several weeks after Tony. As the only two YPs in an escort of 12, we were processed first and taken over to the wings, carrying our kit with us. 'C' wing was our destination. We were given cells next to each other on the YP landing. There were 50 YPs at Wakefield, and all of them had cells on this landing, which wasn't separated in any way from the rest. Wakefield was the only jail in the country where YPs were allowed to mix freely with adult cons.

After we had put our stuff in our cells, Jackie and I set out to explore our new surroundings. The wing was virtually deserted. We were surprised that the screw who had brought us on to the wing had gone off and left us to our own devices.

We wandered down on to the 'ones', the 'threes' and 'fours' above us were just bare landings housing rows of cells. Spread along the 'ones' was a snooker table, two table-tennis tables and several dartboards. None was in use. However, we could imagine that this would be the centre of activity come association time.

Along either side of the 'ones' were messes, where the fellas ate their meals. Each mess was two cells knocked into one and contained a few tables and chairs. Four of the messes were reserved for YPs only. We searched out the number of the mess we had been assigned to and went inside. The only difference from the adult messes was that there was a TV in the corner.

Jackie and I came back out on to the ones and just stood, looking around. In truth, we were a bit bewildered. Back at the Scrubs the screws were on you all the time. Whenever you so much as stuck your head out of your cell, some screw would shout at you. We were surprised at the degree of freedom we seemed to have here. All the time we were half expecting some screw to appear and start shouting at us, demanding to know what we were doing lounging about.

But no screw appeared. We were allowed to explore at will. There were a few cons about, mostly cleaners. One fella came over to us. He was short, very stocky, with a bushy beard and long hair. Through the hair we could discern that he was only in his early 20s. The gold ring in his ear was the finishing touch that made him look something like a pirate. Such studied, irreverent disarray certainly impressed me.

Perhaps he was out to impress. It was obvious from our blue jackets that we were YPs. Within seconds of introducing himself he told us that he was doing double life with a couple of twelves running concurrent. He pointed out others who were also doing long sentences.

I had heard a lot about Wakefield; the cranks and the violence. These fellas who had been singled out to me seemed to be denizens of some strange jungle. I had never met their like before, so I had nothing with which to compare them. They were characters straight out of the Sunday tabloids. It wouldn't be wise to show fear, because someone could take this as an invitation to come on and bully you. However, these were men who had mutilated and butchered like savages, so you couldn't help but fear. I longed for some time to pass so that I would know what was safe and what wasn't in this new and unfamiliar world.

Jackie and I collected our dinners early and went into our allotted mess. We had been there for only a few minutes when we heard the sound of activity out on the wing. The fellas were coming in from work. Suddenly the door burst open, and two YPs bowled in with dinner trays in their hands. They paused, momentarily surprised by the two newcomers in their mess. Recovering quickly, they slammed their trays down on a nearby table, turned the TV on loud, then sat down to eat.

What immediately struck me was their bounce and arrogance. Back at the Scrubs their attitude would have brought them instant trouble from the screws. They were positively flash. And so sure of themselves.

I studied them more closely. Both had specially tailored shirts on, with big, well-starched collars. They wore tight grey trousers, and their blue jackets were pressed with sharp creases.

Most surprising of all, both had long, curly hair with big bushy sideburns. At the Scrubs they would have been prime candidates for the Number One clippers right across the top. They would have emerged from the barbers with a haircut that only began a couple of inches above their ears. I was amazed by the degree of freedom that the YPs seemed to enjoy here.

More YPs came in until there were 12 of us in the same mess. A couple started talking to us, asking where we had come from and telling us about Wakefield. I was still very much on the defensive, but Jackie quickly felt his feet. He wasn't intimidated at all. He had nothing to fear from YPs, no matter how long they were doing. He had held his own with grown men.

By his attitude and manner Jackie began to assert himself. Without saying as much, he let it be known that if anyone wanted a row, then they could have one. Once again I felt reassured that Jackie was my pal.

Over the next couple of weeks we got to know the other YPs and the place. The regime was very relaxed. We could have all sorts of things that were forbidden at the Scrubs. Although we could mix freely with the adults, by and large the YPs kept to themselves. There was a certain degree of elitism in the fact that we were the 50 longest-serving YPs in the country. That didn't mean that we were the toughest, although many clearly thought they were. Their special status had gone to their heads. The authorities were emphasizing that our crimes were too serious for us to mix with others of our age. To the average YP this was just what he wanted to hear. Consequently, the YPs at Wakefield certainly thought they were something special.

In truth, they weren't. They were in for murder, attempted murder and other seriously violent crimes, but these were largely unlucky, one-off affairs. A collection of circumstances and an immature individual carried along on the crest of his passion. A cathartic explosion of violence that was quite out of character. There were scores of young tearaways back at the Scrubs who were tougher and more vicious. Many here were more mental patient than criminal.

Geordie was typical. A baby-faced 16 year old, all quiffed hairstyle and swagger, he had tried to rob an old man in a Durham park. In the process he had knocked him down, kicked him in the head and killed him. Beneath the bravado he was still a bewildered and frightened child, trying to cope with Wakefield.

There was one particularly weird fella, whom Jackie and I referred to as 'Burnt-head'. We never knew his name or his offence, but he was the most frightening thing I had ever seen in my life. Other YPs told us that he had thrown a fit a few years before coming into prison and fallen so that his head ended up in an open fire. It had burned off all one side of his face. He was totally bald, and the skin of his head and face was a mass of angry scar tissue. His nose and left ear had melted down to twisted stubs. The corner of his mouth was turned up in a permanent rictus.

That he should have survived to carry with him forever such a nightmare visage was a tragedy in itself. The greater tragedy was the unseen but undoubted scar on his psyche. Yet whatever crime he had committed, the authorities had seen fit to send him to a prison.

There were other sad cases, many more fool than knave. The only distinction the courts had made was to sentence them to very long terms. Looking around me, I began to consider myself both lucky and blessed.

Jackie soon stood out head and shoulders above all the other YPs. He was like a man amongst boys. He was one of the very few who were married. Without ever throwing a punch he assumed a leading role. Others deferred to him. His opinion was the one that counted. His was the sun around which the other planets rotated.

Tony had come to see us on the first day. He recognized Jackie from the Scrubs, but only knew him vaguely. Jackie largely ignored Tony, regarding him as something of a fool. Despite

Tony's intelligence he had a talent for appearing gormless. He was certainly immature. His high IQ didn't add any sophistication to his adolescent manner. He didn't command much respect amongst the other YPs either.

He was friendly with another YP called Mick. Brummie Mick was doing five for Post Office robberies. He was as immature as Tony, but lacked his intelligence. They were well matched. Both liked to play childish tricks and came out with equally childish remarks. Mick had a bit more credibility amongst the other YPs than Tony, but only just.

Occasionally I could have a sensible conversation with Tony. We were both interested in politics and held right-wing views. I soon came to understand his philosophy and his personality. He was a fan of Nietzsche. He believed devoutly in his concepts of *Mensch* and *Übermensch*. He clearly thought himself to be one of the latter. This gave him rights over and above ordinary men.

Honour and pride were paramount in his value-system. He wasn't particularly courageous or tough, but it was the fact that he thought himself an honourable man that set him above others.

He saw himself as some undiscovered genius who was yet to find his milieu. The objective observer might find it hard to discern some meaningful criteria to support this. In truth, Tony was a highly intelligent but immature young fella, with a painful inferiority complex. Fascism was just the doctrine to allow him to feel superior.

Tony and Mick would often try to hang around with Jackie and me. Sometimes we would tolerate them, sometimes we wouldn't. Gradually they drifted out to the fringes of our circle. We spoke to them, but they weren't friends.

There was another Brummie on the YPs called Roy Aston. He was a tall, rangy fella, doing eight for attempted murder. He was typically in the Northern yobbo vein, with a greased-up Elvis hairstyle and long sideburns. Skin-tight trousers clung to his long, lanky legs. He was aggressive, arrogant and walked with a swagger that owed more to Hollywood than West Bromwich. Until Jackie had arrived, Roy had been the local hardman amongst the YPs.

One look at Jackie, though, convinced him that he'd come a poor second in any punch-up. From then on he went out of his way to be friendly. When you got to know him, though, he wasn't such a bad fella. Much of the swagger was a front, and at least he had the backbone to stand up for himself against the screws. He didn't become a bosom pal of either Jackie or me, but he was often in our company and became a friend of sorts.

After a few weeks I began to feel more at ease at Wakefield, but it was always a bizarre place to me. There were regular violent incidents amongst the adult cons. I was very aware that I was a youth in the company of grown men – and very dangerous ones at that.

My first fear on arrival, and it was a common one amongst the YPs, was of the poofs. There were apocryphal tales of YPs who had been lured into adult cons' cells for coffee, biscuits and a chat but had ended up by being raped. It had also happened in the showers and recesses.

To most proud young men, still measuring their masculinity against that of others, this would be the ultimate indignity. Something so shameful that, had it happened, it would have to be kept secret. Something so dishonourable that, no matter what the consequences, you would have to kill the perpetrator.

My first act, on my very first night at Wakefield, was to make a blade. We were issued with all-steel, round-ended fish knives as part of our cutlery. I spent several hours filing it on the flagstone cell floor until it had a sharp, tapering point. Any poof who came anywhere near me could have some of that.

As the months passed, I quite got to like Wakefield. The

novelty of being treated like an adult by the screws came as a welcome relief after the daily humiliations at the Scrubs. Jackie and I became inseparable. As two young Londoners from the same manor doing time up North, we shared a common background. Neither of us had been that far away from our families before. We were regularly homesick. The cold weather and the Northern accents were a constant reminder that we didn't belong.

We shared our local papers, looking for references to people we knew; just to keep in touch. When we watched *Steptoe* on the TV, the streets of Notting Hill around which it was filmed brought back painful memories. We talked about our families together and read each other's letters. Anything to dispel the sense of isolation that came from being in an alien part of the country.

At about this time I had a falling out with Tony and Mick. I had had a model plane kit sent in. Now, amongst the YPs who thought they were trendy, hobbies and model-making were thoroughly naff pastimes. Only boring people with no pals did hobbies. However, as my mother had gone to the trouble of getting it for me, I decided to make it.

I had neither the patience, nor the practical skills. The resulting model was an abortion of balsa, paper and glue. Its only use was as a talking-point. Several times Jackie, Tony, Mick and I stood around it and laughed. It was an inspired foul-up. A craftsman couldn't have made it that way deliberately.

Tony asked me what I was going to do with it. Jokingly, I said I was going to burn it ritually in the recess: a phoenix that would never fly in life and certainly wouldn't rise from the ashes. In the end I put it on my bookshelf and forgot about it.

Several days later I was coming along the landing towards my cell when I smelled burning. In a world where there was only a limited range of smells, it was instantly noticeable. As I got closer I could see faint wisps of smoke coming from my doorway. I rushed in to find the air thick with smoke. My metal slops bucket was in the middle of the cell and in it the blackened and twisted remains of the plane.

I was instantly very angry. The plane meant nothing to me. I was only going to throw it away anyway, but to burn it in my cell was taking the piss. I immediately guessed who was responsible. It was just the sort of childish prank that Tony would play.

I dumped the bucket in the recess and went looking for him. He must have guessed that I would. I couldn't find him anywhere. By the time a couple of hours had passed and tea-time had arrived, I had calmed down a bit. Nevertheless, I caught him outside his mess and gave him a volley. I called him all the childish, silly bastards I could think of and told him he had taken a liberty. 'Just leave me right out in future,' I said. 'Don't even speak to me.'

Later on, Jackie asked me about it. I told him what had happened, but that it was only a trivial matter and not to worry as I had already dealt with it. He didn't fall out with Tony himself, but he was annoyed with him over it.

The next incident came as a complete surprise to everyone. Ignore it as much as we would, we were constantly aware of the interest of various poofs. There were always a couple hanging around the YP landing. Once they realized you weren't interested, though, most of them would leave you alone.

However, it was all thoroughly disconcerting. Here we were, strutting around like young tough guys, yet well aware that there were those who would fuck us like women if they could. Did the fact that I might arouse those kind of feelings in another man lessen me in some way? Or was it purely a reflection on the other? Most of us resolved this dilemma by arming ourselves with some kind of weapon and staying away from the majority of adult cons.

There was a right raver amongst the YPs though. Coffee was a half-caste male prostitute who worked the Bayswater area. She'd been on the game since she was 15 and was mature and sophisticated beyond her tender years. Not satisfied with merely going with her punters, she had set them up to be robbed. Now, at 19, she was doing a four for robbery with violence.

Coffee was very much in demand at Wakefield. Her young, half-caste features hadn't thickened yet and were framed by a bushy, black Afro that predated the style by several years: a sort of Angela Davis with a twelve o'clock shadow.

Coffee made absolutely no bones about her sexuality and swished about in skin-tight grey trousers. She was highly promiscuous. Although she had many lovers amongst the adult cons, she always went out of her way to try to get hold of other YPs. Youth seemed to hold a powerful fascination for her.

As she came off the same manor as we did, something we shared with no one else at Wakefield, Jackie and I occasionally talked to her. Sometimes we swapped the local papers. We were quite embarrassed, though, by the fact that the only other Notting Hill fella in the jail was a raving poof. We always kept things very formal with Coffee.

The day after I fell out with Tony over my plane, a breath of scandal ran through the YP community. Coffee, usually immaculately turned out, was wandering about with her hair all over the place. From her face and general demeanour she looked like the cat who had been out on the tiles all night. Never one to keep a secret, she let it be known that she'd had a steamy session with Tony.

People were amazed. It definitely wasn't the done thing. If Tony had had much standing amongst the YPs it would have damaged it considerably. As it was, it just confirmed in people's minds that he was a bit of a berk.

A couple of days later an incident happened between Jackie on the one hand, and Tony and Mick on the other. Jackie was sitting in their mess when Mick walked by and accidentally knocked against a table. A cup of water standing near the edge tipped over into Jackie's lap. It was a pure accident, but, in their typically silly manner, Tony and Mick started smirking about it.

Jackie left to change his trousers, annoyed not so much by

the soaking as by their laughing about it. When he came back Tony was lounging in the doorway, but Mick wasn't in the mess. Jackie asked Tony where Mick was. Tony said he didn't know. As Jackie turned away, he saw Mick standing in the doorway of a mess opposite. He was right in Tony's line of sight, and he had obviously known where he was when Jackie had asked.

Angry now, Jackie spun around and punched Tony in the face, sending him flying backwards into the mess. Jackie hurried across the 'ones' and, as Mick backed away, he followed, punching him several times to the head and body. Then he walked away, back up to his cell on the 'twos'.

Neither Tony nor Mick was hurt, but both were severely embarrassed. It meant a considerable loss of face for them in the eyes of the other YPs. They weren't held in much esteem anyway, although they liked to think they were.

The truly amazing thing about the incident was that I didn't get to hear about it. It wasn't surprising that Jackie didn't tell me, because he wouldn't want to get me involved. He was always one to sort out his own trouble without dragging in his mates. And he knew that I already had the hump with Tony. It was common knowledge amongst many of the other YPs, though, but nobody mentioned it to me. Perhaps they assumed that I already knew.

In retrospect, my ignorance of the incident was a crucial factor in what was subsequently to happen. Knowing Tony like I did, I might have realized how this would have shattered his already fragile ego. I could have guessed how his mind would have seethed in a whirlpool of destructive emotion. The already parlous state of his self-esteem would be further damaged. His self-image as an honourable man could hardly square with being attacked and doing nothing about it. Coming on top of the exposure of his embarrassing liaison with Coffee, no doubt he felt that there was only one thing he could do.

• • •

Tony and Mick made an elaborate plan to kill Jackie. They got spare overalls from the clothing store in which to do it. They had a knife and an iron bar made in the foundry. They knew Jackie played football at the weekend. They planned to jump him in his cell after the match.

It was Saturday afternoon, and Jackie was playing for the prison against an outside team. I stood on the sportsfield watching the match, with two pals of ours from another wing. Benny and Squiz were recently made-up YPs. Now given adult status they had moved on to 'A' wing. We still managed to see them, though, on the yard and in the workshops.

After the game the three of us talked to Jackie as he came off. He hurried away to take a shower and I walked to the centre with Benny and Squiz. We stood talking for a while.

Tony and Mick saw Jackie come in. They had been watching out for him from the 'threes'. They saw him collect his clothes and washing gear from his cell, then head downstairs towards the showers.

They slipped down to the 'twos' and went along the landing towards Jackie's cell. They walked as nonchalantly as possible, because directly below on the 'ones' sat dozens of cons watching a communal TV set. Anyone looking up would see them, but they were engrossed in their programme. No one saw them slip into Jackie's cell, pulling the door to behind them.

Jackie took a quick shower. It wasn't long before tea-time, and he had things to do. He dried himself, dressed, then headed back upstairs with a towel around his neck. His tired body invigorated by the hot water, he bowled along the landing and strode into his cell.

Mick and Tony were hiding behind the door. As Jackie came in, Mick hit him across the forehead with a massive iron bar. His forward momentum caused him to fall headlong on to the stone-slabbed floor. Tony was on him immediately. In an action replay of Crawley, he repeatedly stabbed him in the back.

Jackie had no chance. There was a shouted cry of pain, then the heavy thud of a body falling to the floor. It alerted some of the TV watchers below. As Tony and Mick slipped out of Jackie's cell, several pairs of eyes watched them go.

They hurried off, each to his own cell. There they changed into clean clothes. Their old ones they dropped into the laundry basket at the end of the landing. Then they went to sit in their mess.

I finished talking to Benny and Squiz on the centre. Calling my goodbyes I turned on to 'C' wing and headed along the 'twos' towards my cell. I had only gone a few yards when I noticed that Roy's cell, which was at the start of the 'twos', had its flag sticking out. He had obviously rung his bell to be let out.

It was unusual that he was locked in at all. It was Saturday afternoon, and everyone was allowed to be out on association. Even if he didn't want to come out, he could have sat in his cell with the door pulled to. He didn't have to lock himself in. Sometimes people did bang themselves up, though, usually when they didn't want company. However, Roy was often moody, so it wasn't entirely out of character.

I stopped in his doorway and looked through the spy-hole. Loud rock music was playing inside, and Roy was dancing about and singing. I shouted to him through the spy-hole. He immediately stopped and came over to the door. He shouted for me to get a screw and let him out.

I turned from his door and was surprised to see a screw hurrying towards me from the direction of my cell. Usually you could never find a screw when you wanted one, especially just before tea on a Saturday afternoon.

It was one of our regular landing screws. 'Open Roy's door please, Boss,' I said, stepping out in front of him.

What happened next seemed to take place very quickly, almost in a blur. I briefly noticed a shocked, panic-stricken look on the screw's face, as he rushed by.

'I can't,' he said breathlessly. 'Someone's bashed your mate Jackie.' With that, he thrust something into my hands and was past me.

Until then I hadn't even noticed he was carrying anything. I looked down and saw that I was holding a massive iron bar. It was easily as thick as my arm, curled at the end like a shepherd's crook.

I turned to say something, but he was gone, running towards the centre. I felt the cold grip of fear in my stomach. What had happened to Jackie that had frightened him so badly? One instinct compelled me to run the other way; another told me that Jackie was in trouble, and I should go to help him. As I rushed towards his cell I could hear Roy shouting, 'What's happening,' from behind his door.

At a run now I reached Jackie's door and plunged inside. What I saw brought me up short. Jackie was lying face up on the floor, in the middle of the cell. A widening pool of blood spread around his head like some fiery halo.

I threw the iron bar into a corner and bent over him. There was a deep dent in his forehead where the knob of the bar had sunk in. This was the source of all the blood I could see. Next to him was a long, bloody skid-mark where his head had first made contact with the stone floor.

He was coughing, trying to get his breath. Gurgled, indistinct words came from his mouth.

'What is it, Jackie? Who did it?' I asked urgently. 'Before the screws come back, who did this to you? We'll do the fuckers.'

'Can't breathe, can't breathe,' was all he could mumble in reply.

I noticed he had his tie on, although it wasn't done up tight. It was the only reason I could see for his breathing difficulties. I loosened it right off and unbuttoned the top buttons of his shirt.

Still he kept mumbling, 'Can't breathe, can't breathe.' If I had known that Tony was involved, I might have guessed at the stab wounds in his back, the ones that were causing his lungs to fill, slowly drowning him in his own blood.

Suddenly, the door burst open. The Chief and several screws crowded into the cell, with them the landing screw who had thrust the bar at me.

'Out,' said the Chief. 'Get out.' I tried to protest that Jackie was my pal and that I should stay with him, but I was hustled unceremoniously from the cell.

As I was pushed out, I noticed Roy in the ruck of curious faces outside the door. Some screw had obviously let him out of his cell. He was shouting, 'Who's done my mate Jackie?'

I grabbed his arm. Pulling him along the landing I whispered, 'Quick, let's try to find out who did it before the screws bang us all up.' Stirrings of revenge were gradually replacing my original feelings of fear and concern.

'I've heard that Scouse fella Purdin saw something,' said Roy excitedly.

'We'll need a tool in case they're still about,' I said. I ducked into my cell to collect my sharpened fish knife, then rushed downstairs towards the YP messes.

Purdin was a YP like us. He shared the same mess as Tony and Mick. As we hurried in, we saw him sitting at a table in the corner. Sitting at another table was Mick. There was no sign of Tony.

Roy and I towered over Purdin threateningly. He was a scrawny-looking fella who was forever moaning about something or other. Now he sat silently, his pasty face white with fear.

'Who did you see come out of Jackie's cell?' I demanded, holding my knife so he could see it.

'I didn't see anything, I swear,' he said, frightened and panicky. Later on I would muse on the irony of one of the attackers sitting across the room from us as we ordered Purdin to tell us who did it.

In the background I could hear the sound of the screws

coming round and ordering everyone away to their cells. I put the knife back in my pocket and slipped out of the mess.

There were screws everywhere, shepherding men from the messes and away to their cells. There was a lot of moaning, but the cons knew it had to be something serious. I went up to my cell and banged the door behind me. As I went in, I noticed that Jackie's door was banged up too. They had obviously taken him somewhere.

I sat down and thought about what had just happened. How had lightning struck so close to home yet again? Once more I was in the middle of a very violent situation. Someone had seriously hurt Jackie. It was a bad injury, but he was a tough fella. I reasoned that, inside a week, he would be back with a bandage around his head. Then the fella who had done it had better watch out. For if he had needed an iron bar to do Jackie in the first place, he wouldn't stand much chance when Jackie caught him man to man.

I puzzled over who could have done it. The jail was full of dangerous cranks. A few angry words could make a mortal enemy. Perhaps Jackie had said something to someone. Perhaps it was an argument from the football match. There were so many possibilities and no hard evidence. For the time being all I could do was sit and think about it.

To be banged up so early on a Saturday was unusual. It disrupted my normal routine. I had specific things I did when I was banged up after evening association. I would have to find something to occupy myself with now.

I got my guitar out and started to play. I often played to relieve tension, although I was no great musician. I banged away, more with nervous energy than skill.

In the background I could hear fellas shouting out of their windows to each other, asking what was going on. Occasionally I stopped to listen. I heard one fella say that the police were going from cell to cell interviewing people.

The thought suddenly struck me that my prints were all over the iron bar in Jackie's cell. I had his blood on me too. I had heard tales about how thick the local Old Bill were. I was already doing a sentence for manslaughter. I pondered the possibility of being fitted up.

But the screw had given me the bar, and he would remember. Benny and Squiz would confirm that I had been with them on the centre. And when Jackie came round he would say that it wasn't me. However, the circumstances were enough to make me view the coming police interview with trepidation.

From time to time I heard the dull crash of doors opening and closing. Finally my door opened and in came two local CID. They pushed the door to, sat down and introduced themselves. They seemed friendly enough, but I was very much on my guard.

They said that they understood I was Jackie's closest pal and that I had known him outside. I confirmed this, and they nodded in unison, as if satisfied that they were making a concrete start. Then they asked me who could have done it.

Now I was in an awkward position. Even if I had known, I couldn't have told them. I wasn't going to grass anyone, in spite of the fact that they had done my pal. And Jackie would support me in this. He wouldn't want the help of the Old Bill. As soon as he came back we would sort it out ourselves. However, I didn't want to sound too uncooperative.

I had been sitting on my bed, lounging against the wall. I leaned forward and said earnestly, 'Look, I honestly don't know who did it. It's a complete mystery to me. The first thing I heard about it was when the screw told me.'

They both paused and looked at each other. Nothing was said, but I could read the look: another brick in the wall of silence. As if coming to some unspoken conclusion they both turned to me, and one said, 'Well, we're not going to mess about with you. You might as well know. Jackie's dead.'

Quite involuntarily my hands flew up to my face, as a wave

of shock and grief gripped me. I couldn't believe it. Jackie, so full of life and spirit. So tough and capable. It seemed inconceivable that he was gone and wouldn't be coming back.

Then other thoughts pushed into my consciousness. What about his wife and young baby? What would my mother think when she heard that Jackie had been murdered in the very next cell to mine? She was already under pressure. This would really worry her. Finally, what about me?

I was in a weird, Agatha Christie type situation now. Someone had murdered my best pal in the cell right next door. I didn't have a clue who had done it. What would happen if the police didn't get them, and everyone was unlocked again? Would they come after me next, thinking that, as Jackie's pal, I would come after them? It wouldn't be so bad if I knew who they were. At least I could keep an eye on them and be on my guard if they came close. I could strike first if necessary. But it could be anyone.

Every time I went to the toilet, used the shower or went into my cell alone, I would have to be on my guard. I would make my own enquiries. I'd have to. But what a way to have to live. There was nowhere to hide. I was locked in with the killers like a mouse locked up with a cat. I found myself secretly hoping that the police would get them, then felt instantly guilty at the thought.

The two CID were still sitting there looking at me. Only a few seconds had passed. 'Look,' I said in a voice that was more like a croak, 'I really don't know who did it. Jackie never said anything to me about falling out with anyone.'

I told them about speaking to Jackie after the game. I explained that he had gone off for a shower whilst I stood talking on the centre. I mentioned speaking to Roy, who was banged up. At this point they stopped me. They seemed very interested at the mention of Roy.

I paused, thinking carefully about what I was saying. I didn't want to drop anyone in it, but surely the fact that Roy was locked in cleared him of suspicion. He was a bit saucy to the screws and had probably told the Old Bill to piss off. Perhaps they just had it in for him. Anyway, he was our pal. It was only right that I should alibi him, especially as it was true.

They asked what he was doing. 'Just dancing about to the music,' I said, and no, there didn't seem to be anything suspicious in his actions. Clearly, they would have liked more, but there was no more. I moved on to tell of the screw thrusting the bar on me and my running to Jackie's cell and finding him.

Both the CID made notes as I talked. Neither commented on what I had said. Finally they showed me what they had written and asked me to sign it. I didn't consider that I had said anything of value to them. Further, it should clear Roy of suspicion. I signed.

Their leaving merely emphasized the seriousness of my predicament. I was on my own and would have to deal with the problem on my own. There was always Roy. He had come with me to try and find out who had done Jackie, immediately after I had been thrown out of his cell. Then there were a couple of Londoners amongst the YPs with whom Jackie and I had been friendly.

Now we were talking about murder though. Perhaps they wouldn't want to know. You soon found out who your real friends were in situations like this. And irrespective of whatever help I had, as Jackie's pal I would be in the frontline.

I played my guitar again, but now morbid and melancholy. I was too tense to read. Outside you would get drunk, seek the support of your family or console the relatives and share the burden of your grief. Here I could only brood about it in solitude.

Later that evening the screws brought around cocoa. Nothing was said, so it looked like we would remain banged up for the rest of the day. I didn't mind at all. I wasn't hiding, but at least it would give me more time to figure out what I was going to do. As I wrestled with sleep that night, my mind was full of the images of the day.

The following morning everyone was unlocked for breakfast

as usual. I assumed that the police investigation was over. Keeping my sharpened fish knife in my pocket, I slipped out of my cell and headed towards Roy's. Everyone was out on the landings swapping gossip, trying to find out exactly what had happened.

Half-way along the landing I bumped into Coffee. 'They've got Tony, Mick and Roy down the block for it,' she blurted out, an expression of surprise and shock mingled on her face. She put her hand on my arm in an act of concern, no doubt also showing where her sympathies lay following her recent liaison with Tony.

I carried on to find Hutch, a young London pal of ours. He was leaning on the landing rail just outside his door. We grabbed each other by the shoulders, our faces contorted with emotion. 'The fucking slags,' he said, 'they could only do him on the sly.'

Hutch said that Scouse Purdin had seen Tony and Mick come out of Jackie's cell. He had made a statement. There were other witnesses, too, who had seen other things. But we couldn't figure out where Roy fitted in. He had no obvious grouse against Jackie, unless he had always resented being knocked off the number one spot by his arrival. He had been friendly right up to the last. If he were involved, then it was the worst kind of treachery imaginable. But I couldn't believe he was. I had seen him banged up. The Old Bill had obviously made a mistake. Perhaps they had segregated him to put pressure on. Maybe they would let him up after a few days.

The fellas in general were angry over what had happened. Jackie was well liked. They admired his spirit. They didn't like the cowardly way it had been done either. If Tony and Mick had come back on the wing they would have been immediately set about.

I wasn't pleased that they had been grassed, but it certainly resolved a problem for me. If in fact it was them, they would have been looking for an opportunity to do me too. They couldn't afford to take the chance that I would make a come-back.

Eventually I would have heard something. The ensuing tear-up would have been very serious, especially with Tony. Yes, although I wouldn't say as much, I was quite relieved at the outcome.

That afternoon I had a surprise visit. I was taken over to the gate lodge, which was very unusual. As the screw ushered me in, I was surprised to see the Governor, and behind him my sister and Teddy, Jackie's eldest brother.

My sister ran forward and threw her arms around me. Tears were running down her face. Teddy appeared at her side. Grabbing me by the arm, he pulled me to one side. His face was tight and white with shock. His eyes had the staring madness of uncontrollable grief and rage.

'Who did it? Who the fuck did it?' he growled, his voice breaking with emotion. He had been very close to Jackie. I explained that I only knew what I had heard. That there were three fellas down the block for it. But that it was all a mystery to me because I wasn't aware that Jackie had fallen out with anybody.

The Governor hovered in the background as the three of us huddled together. My sister was clinging to me, crying helplessly. I hadn't been aware that the relationship had meant that much to her. It had been over for some time.

What was already a heavy situation for me was rapidly turning into a tragedy of classic proportions. Once again I mused on the way that bizarre happenings increasingly seemed to be a part of my life.

After about an hour, Teddy and my sister left. It was a draining experience for me. They could take their grief outside with them, to dissipate in the distractions of freedom. I would sit and mull over mine like a miser.

Everything that came afterwards was a distinct anticlimax. I missed Jackie's company and the security of his friendship. Then there were the comings and goings of the police. Few of the fellas would tolerate a grass. Jackie was well liked, though, so they didn't feel like having a go at those who had grassed the three down the block. They just ignored them.

Several days later I was called in for a police interview. I was in a very awkward position now. If I actively sabotaged the prosecution case and Tony and Mick got off, Jackie's family and my sister would never forgive me. However, I wasn't going to do them any damage in court, even if Jackie was my best pal. I would settle things in my own way or not at all.

The police had my statement with them. They read it through to me, including the bit about my finding Roy banged up. It didn't do anyone any harm. I wasn't putting anyone in it. It didn't even mention Tony or Mick. And as far as Roy was concerned, it placed him well away from the action.

I still couldn't believe he'd had anything to do with it. I'd heard no rumours concerning his involvement. In fact I was pleased to give that piece of evidence for him. Anyway, it was the truth.

At first I thought I was wanted as a defence witness. That would have been embarrassing for me in the eyes of Jackie's family. It might look like treachery or even that I was involved in some way. The police reassured me that, as mine was all uncontested evidence, in the circumstances I would be listed as part of the prosecution's case. I acquiesced at this not-too-ideal a solution. They would only subpoena me anyway, so I had little choice really.

Several months passed, and people largely forgot about the killing. Tony, Mick and Roy had all long since been moved to Leeds. The trial was scheduled for Leeds Assizes.

One morning about 12 of us were called over to reception. There were five YPs including Purdin. The rest were adult cons. I didn't have a clue who was saying what, but I did know that we were both defence and prosecution witnesses mixed. It had all turned very sour. I didn't feel like talking; I just wanted to get it over with.

A van took us to Leeds Assizes, and we were lodged in cells beneath the courts. I waited for several hours before I was called. I climbed some stairs and, to my surprise, came right up in the back of the dock. Tony, Mick and Roy were sitting with their backs to me, so close that I could have touched them.

I was led over to the witness box. Any court appearance is always an intimidating experience, but the massive chamber of Leeds Assizes was especially so.

As I stood there nervously, I glanced at the dock. Tony was lolling in his chair, sullenly arrogant, with a sour smirk on his face. He had the air of someone who was largely indifferent to the goings-on. However, I could tell that beneath this studied indifference he was enjoying every minute of it.

This was his personal statement. Anyone who messed with him would end up dead. Murder was a statistically unusual act in the early Sixties, yet Tony had done two in less than a year.

Mick was sitting there all pasty faced and afraid. He was only doing a five; a life sentence would be a disaster for him. He definitely wasn't enjoying the proceedings.

Roy was moving restlessly in his chair. It was as if he were having trouble sitting still. He looked outraged, disgusted and frightened all at the same time. Even knowing what I did, it was apparent that he felt he shouldn't be there.

My part was over very quickly. Defence counsel questioned me in detail about my finding Roy locked up. He emphasized the part where I had said that he didn't seem agitated or unusual in any way. Before I knew it, I was back downstairs in the cells again.

Later on a screw came to my cell. I was surprised when he told me that all three had been found guilty. Tony had stood, still arrogant, as the judge put on the black cap. He had committed two separate murders within the space of a year, which made it a capital offence. He smiled as he was sentenced to death.

Mick stood, cowed and pale, as he was sentenced to life. Roy couldn't contain himself. 'I'm not fucking guilty,' he had shouted as he was also sentenced to life.

Jackie had a big funeral in Notting Hill. There was a long cortège of cars and hundreds of wreaths. A large crowd attended the burial. The manor had turned out in force to send off one of its sons in style. It was extensively reported in the local papers. Yet again I felt a part of local history. To step out of the crowd once was unusual: to make repeated appearances was bizarre.

After a few weeks Tony's death sentence was commuted to life imprisonment. It would run together with his previous HMP. Several months later the three appeals came up. At the last moment Tony and Mick abandoned theirs and gave evidence for Roy. By now another alibi witness had appeared for him. His sentence was quashed. As his other sentence had already finished, he was released.

There was a rumour that, a year or so later, a group of Jackie's friends had slipped up to Birmingham and done Roy. It was said he was seriously stabbed and is now in a wheelchair.

After a few years in Security Wings, Mick spent the rest in normal jails. He was released after about 15 years.

Tony spent many years in Security Wings. He worked out assiduously on the weights and turned his skinny build into a massive physique. He studied on the Open University and got a First Class Honours degree. He was released after 20 years. He was last heard of living in the West Country, sharing a flat with several cats. On a couple of occasions he was invited to lecture on penal matters.

13. The Albany Wall Game

HAD BEEN in the chokey at Albany for over two months. The original 56 days' solitary for my escape attempt (described in Chapter 13 of my first book, *Parkhurst Tales*) had passed. My situation hadn't changed, though, because on the day it finished, I was put on Rule 43 for 'subversive activity'.

If I hadn't been used to the perverse workings of the system already, perhaps this would have surprised me. After all, how could I be subversive in solitary confinement? Who could I possibly subvert, other than myself?

In reality it was just a ploy to keep me in the chokey. The situation up on the wings was still supposed to be volatile. However, the number of incidents had fallen. I suppose the Governor wasn't taking any chances though. He wasn't going to allow me back up, or the other 15 or so who were in the chokey with me.

After the madness of the early days of the riot following my escape attempt and subsequent crackdown, life in the chokey had settled down to a steady war of attrition. Things weren't tranquil by any means. We still had regular organized protests, but we no longer stayed up every single night, banging and shouting to keep the screws awake in the nearby quarters.

There were still nights when this did happen. We lit fires and smashed up, when we had anything to burn or break, but protests were organized more around particular objectives.

We weren't going to accept being kept in indefinite solitary under Rule 43. We realized that the worst thing we could do was sit quietly in our cells. That way the Governor would be under no pressure to do anything about the situation. We would be left for months and months, possibly years.

Ironically, although Rule 43 wasn't classed as a punishment, it was far worse than being on ordinary chokey. Admittedly, we didn't have to put our bedding out each morning and sit or lie on a hard surface all day. Also, we could have books, newspapers and spend our canteen, if we had any.

But at least with punishment you knew how long you had to do. It was always a fixed term of days, and never more than 56, except in exceptional circumstances. With Rule 43, though, it was open ended. You never knew how long you had to do.

We would only be let up when the Governor said so and not before. There was no appeal. In the first place they never told you any specific reason why you were on 'subversive'. This made it impossible to formulate any challenge to the decision.

Secondly, the only people you could appeal to were the VC, and mostly they automatically rubber-stamped the Governor's rulings. So all we could do was perform. We tried to create as much disruption as possible.

There were 20 cells in the chokey. Half a dozen were kept empty for normal punishments, those who would leave the chokey after they had done their time. The rest held us 'so-called' rioters.

Immediately behind the chokey stood 'E' wing. This had been used as a segregation block too. There were still 20 or so fellas held there on Rule 43. When they joined in with us on a protest, it could be both noisy and effective.

Strangely enough, many of the chokey screws had some sympathy with us. The Governor had deliberately manned the chokey with older, more decent screws, well knowing that if he put the heavy mob in, it would be off all the time.

We didn't feel any sympathy for them though. The pressure of trying to survive each day in solitary filled us with a hatred of anything in a uniform. They were grown men. They knew what they were doing. They had seen plenty of men crack up in solitary, kill themselves even. They were as guilty as the rest.

However, there was never any brutality by them. They didn't go out of their way to wind us up. We got what we were entitled to, so we never aimed our protests specifically at them.

Whether this was any consolation was doubtful. They were always the ones subject to the most noise, the immediate effects of disruption and all the ensuing stress. It couldn't have been easy for them, working in the chokey.

Much of their restraint was due to an SO we called Punchy. He was a rugged, stocky fella of about 40 who had once been a boxer. He was tough, fair and could handle himself. There was no brutality whilst he was on duty.

You could see that he was disturbed by a lot that went on, especially the brutality by the heavy mob up in the wings. Being straightforward himself, he resented the Governor's underhanded ways. He wasn't on our side by any means, but if it had been left to him we could have sorted out our grievances without having to perform.

Up on the wings most of the resistance had died down. All the rebels had been removed to the chokey, and the rest had been intimidated by the heavy mob.

There were a group of about a dozen of the latter. All were big fellas, most were ex-services. They went out of their way to provoke people. On a spin, they would rip the cell to pieces leaving possessions all over the floor. They would confiscate things for no reason. Remarks were made about wives and girlfriends.

The regime was very restrictive, with fellas being let out of their cells only for short periods. Any sign of rebellion would be met with instant violence. Several screws would jump on the fella and carry him bodily to the chokey. All the way there he would be punched, kicked and beaten. Then they would throw him naked into a strip cell, where he would be left for the night.

The following day he would find that he had been charged with assault. On the subsequent VC he would lose from six months upwards, coupled with 56 days' solitary. It was an effective method of intimidation. Apart from our continued detention on Rule 43, this brutality was the main thing we protested about.

I was in a cell on the outward-facing side of the chokey. There were nine cells on this side, all looking out towards the perimeter fence. The first cell was kept for punishments that came and went. I was in the next cell down.

One morning I heard the first cell door open, then slam. I realized that they had just put someone in there. I went to my window and called out. Within seconds the fella came to his window and answered.

It was Rob, a Scots fella I knew. He told me he had just got seven days for verballing a screw. Then he told me that Joe Mason, a good friend of mine, had just arrived.

Joe and I were very close pals. We kept in constant contact and knew each other's families on the outside. My pleasure at his being in the same jail was tempered with sadness that he had come to a place that was having so much trouble.

Like me, Joe was doing a life sentence from which he would be lucky ever to get out. He was far more notorious, though, having been involved in riots and escapes in several jails. He was powerfully built, a leader of men and was held in universal respect by the fellas. Consequently, the authorities feared him.

I couldn't see him lasting long on the wings. Even if he didn't quickly fall out with some of the screws, he would probably come down the chokey in solidarity with me and the rest of the fellas.

By coincidence I was soon due to go up to the Education Department for a final tutorial before an important OU exam.

The tutor had specifically asked that I should be present. They could hardly bring her down the block to me. They would have to take me up to her class. I just might get the chance to see Joe.

The Education Department lay along one side of a central corridor. On the other side were the entrances to the various wings. The following morning a screw escorted me from the chokey, past the wings and into the classroom.

Here he left me. I wasn't on my own. There was the tutor in the class and a screw standing out in the corridor. There weren't too many places I could go.

At mid-morning the class broke off for a tea-break. There was no hot water available in the Education Department, so the fellas went back to their wings. I had anticipated this and had brought a cup with me.

I left the class with all the others. The screw in the corridor didn't notice me, so I walked on to 'C' wing where I knew Joe was. As I stood at the urn filling my cup, I asked a fella to slip upstairs and fetch him.

Suddenly I heard a shout. Joe came hurrying towards me, a broad smile on his face. We hugged each other and quickly exchanged our news. We knew we didn't have long.

He told be how he had just been thrown out of his last jail. I gave him a brief history of the present trouble at Albany. I asked him to stay out of it if he could, but from the way he looked at me I knew that he wouldn't be able to.

By now several minutes had passed. If I didn't return to the class soon the screw would come looking for me. There could be an argument, which might involve Joe. I decided to get back. As I left the wing Joe called after me, 'Take care, Norm. Be seeing you.' It sounded all too prophetic.

The following morning Joe was down the chokey. One of the fellas stopped at my door and told me that he was in the end cell on the inward-facing side of the chokey. He had volleyed a screw.

From the sound of it he was just looking for an excuse to get down here with us.

Even though Joe was only a short distance away, I was unlikely ever to see him. He would go on exercise with the fellas in the two cells nearest to him. We were only unlocked singly at other times. We would never meet.

Luckily, Punchy was on duty. I knew there was an empty cell next to Joe's. I rang my bell and asked him if I could move. Perhaps because things had been relatively quiet that week, he agreed. He would live to regret it.

Whereas the cell I had just left looked outwards to the fence, my new cell looked inwards on to a small rectangular exercise yard. It was totally enclosed. There were cells running along two adjoining sides. On the other two sides there were blank brick walls about ten feet high.

There wasn't much of a view. In the recent past, though, it had been possible to talk to whoever was on exercise and shout across to the line of cells that ran at right angles to ours.

To the powers that be, though, that must have detracted from the principle of solitary confinement. So they built two breeze-block screening walls, six feet from each line of cells and running parallel to them.

They stood barely seven-foot high, topped with a few strands of barbed wire. There was a flimsy, mesh gate at the end of each wall, to prevent fellas from walking behind them and talking to the occupants of the cells. They served no real function, except to block our line of sight. Now our cells looked out on to a blank grey wall.

There were five cells on our side. Joe was in the end cell, adjoining the brick wall. I was now in the next one up. The third was occupied by a young Irish fella. He had only been down the chokey for a few days, and no one knew anything about him.

Blackie, in the fourth cell, was a short, dark-haired fella in his late 30s, doing a 14 for numerous armed robberies. He was well known in the system and had been involved in various bits of trouble elsewhere.

Blackie was quite a character, with a lively sense of humour. He sported a big, incongruous-looking handlebar moustache. If you hadn't known he was a bank robber, you could have been forgiven for mistaking him for an RAF Group Captain. He wouldn't have looked out of place in any wartime aircrew.

Next to him was Jeff, a wild young Canadian fella who was game for anything. He was only doing an eight, but his relatively early release date didn't stop him from getting involved in protests. He had short, cropped, blond hair and a fresh, open face. His salient quality was loyalty. He would never leave a mate in the lurch.

The screws' office was next to Jeff's. It stood at the right angle, between the two lines of inward-facing cells. On the other side of it was the gate that led into the yard. Then there was the second line of cells leading down to the recess and strip cells.

The office was as big as two normal cells. It was constantly occupied by the half-dozen screws who usually manned the chokey. Its back wall was Jeff's side wall. He could hear them as they moved about in there.

It hadn't taken me long to move in. My possessions amounted to only a cardboard box containing a bag of sugar, a few books and a wad of letters held together by an elastic band. The cell, of course, was identical to the one I had just left. The only difference was that the bedboard had been torn from the wall, its hinges hanging loose at the back. Some bricks had been removed from around the window reveal, exposing the gap of the cavity wall.

Dropping my box on the bedboard, I went straight to the window and called to Joe. He came to his window. It had been over two years since we had last spoken at any length. I had been out then and used to bring his wife up to visit him. We had a lot to talk about.

Exercise time came around, and fellas were allowed on to the yard three at a time. Over on the outward-facing side I had always been out with Aussie and Gary, the fellas in the adjoining cells. Now I would go out with two new neighbours.

My turn eventually came, and I walked from my cell into the corridor. The screw then unlocked Joe, but that only made two of us. He had gone past the young Paddy. He must have already exercised with two others. I was well pleased. Now the next one out would be Danny. He was in the end cell on the outward-facing side, directly across the corridor from Joe.

This was a double bonus. Not only was Danny one of our own but he was also on the outward-facing side. This meant that if we wanted to get a message across to the fellas on that side, we could now do so secretly by telling Danny. We could always have shouted across, but then the screws would have heard too.

Danny hurried towards Joe and warmly shook his hand. They had been in some trouble at Hull together, so they already shared a bond. Danny's pale, drawn face lit up in a smile as he walked out on exercise with us.

Danny came from the North of Scotland. He had been an unlikely robber. But his irrepressible spirit and rebellious nature didn't lend itself easily to menial farm work. He had drifted south to Glasgow and got in with some robbers who operated south of the border. His 12 was a long sentence for those times and that part of the country.

In prison his rebelliousness and loyalty to others soon got him into trouble. He was moved to Dartmoor, a hard jail for troublemakers. Here he had several severe beatings and long spells of solitary. His spirit wouldn't let him give in, though, but it seriously affected his health.

Now, four years into his sentence, his tall frame was painfully thin. His natural 14 stone was down to ten. His face was gaunt, with eyes sunk deep into their sockets. It had affected his mental health too. He had a lost, distant look about him. His attention span was short, and he could easily lose track of a conversation. He regularly took large doses of whatever drugs the sick-bay would give him.

His spirit still burned within him, though, but not so brightly. He still had that faithful, doglike loyalty to others. He wouldn't hesitate to get involved, but now his judgement was suspect. He was easily led. He would loyally follow those who didn't deserve it. His real friends constantly tried to protect him from this. He was regarded with genuine affection by all the chaps.

The three of us walked around the yard in the bright sunlight. Fellas called out to Joe from behind the breeze-block wall. Blackie was an old friend. Stan, Jim and Ernie, also old pals, shouted greetings from the opposite side. Others joined in. If Joe had needed to it made him feel more at home. It was good for our solidarity too.

Solidarity was very important to us. Few of us knew each other on the outside. All we had in common was our shared situation, our rebelliousness and, generally speaking, a London background.

All of us were spirited and hated the oppression of the screws. The only thing they seemed to understand was that which they ruled by: fear and violence. Well, we were no strangers to violence ourselves. The odds were always heavily in their favour, usually in the order of eight to one. But we had the greater courage, coupled with a self-destructiveness born of the desperation caused by an endless sentence.

An attack on one of us was an attack on all. Although we couldn't join in physically, we would smash on our doors with fists, boots and chairs. If one were punished, others would do the same to be punished likewise. Those on bread and water shared the food of those on normal diets.

We supported each other in every way we could. Joint action was our answer to individual isolation. It was the only way that we had a chance of winning. It was the only action that would force their hand. In the paralysing loneliness of solitary, our loyalty to each other was the only thing that kept us going.

Joe's arrival gave us a much needed boost. I had already been something of a leader in my own right. To put the two of us together was a definite mistake.

Exercise finished, and we returned to our cells. You could see that Danny was reluctant to go. His loyalty was tinged with sentimentality. He was so pleased to see his old friend Joe, and he resented the return to solitary.

I walked into my cell, banging the door behind me. I slipped off my shoes and padded over to the window in my stockinged feet. The concrete floor was cool after walking in circles around a small yard for half an hour.

I called to Joe, and he came to his window. For a while we talked of Danny. Of how he would always stand by you right to the end. He had already taken so much stick. 'We must try to keep him out of things as much as we can,' said Joe.

This brought us to the inevitable subject. 'What do you fancy doing, Joe?' I asked. 'If we just sit here, Footer will really take his pound of flesh and keep us here indefinitely.'

Joe had already met Footer that morning on adjudication. He was a poor Governor by any standards. A short, fat, balding man in his middle 50s, he was hardly an imposing figure in a world where physical prowess was everything.

He had a partially crippled leg and walked with the assistance of a wooden cane. He could often be seen pegging about the jail in a shapeless tweed jacket, constantly mopping his florid face with a large off-white handkerchief.

He wasn't an evil man by any means. He was no sadist and didn't seem to take any pleasure in our suffering. He was just weak. He was caught between the pressure of the POA to cut back on privileges and our demands for better conditions.

The POA were always the stronger lobby though. Concessions to us were always made grudgingly, knowing he would have to justify them at the next meeting with the POA. If he had possessed more character and courage he could have asserted himself.

Consequently, we despised him. When your every waking moment is a nightmare of tension as you grapple with the terminal boredom of unending solitary, it is largely academic whether you are there by the express intention of the Governor or merely because he has been forced into it by the POA.

We knew his weakness though. He could be intimidated. This gave us our plan. We would increase the violence of our protests until our pressure exceeded that of the POA. We had nothing to lose. Indefinite solitary would eventually affect our sanity. The strongest mind would crack in the end. So, rather than wait passively, we might as well go down fighting.

Joe took a long time to answer my question. I was beginning to think that he had wandered away from the window and hadn't heard me. 'I don't want to commit myself to anything at the moment,' he said quietly. 'If I say something, I'll have to do it. But I haven't had time to weigh the situation up yet. We'll talk about it tonight.'

That was fair enough. After all, although he had been in the jail a couple of days, he had only been in the chokey a few hours. He would have to consider the various options and the support each was likely to get from the rest of the fellas.

We made desultory conversation for a while. All the time others were coming out for exercise. Looking along the alleyway between the breeze-block wall and our cells, we could see the gate that led into the yard. As fellas came through we would catch a brief glimpse of them. There were quick waves and short, shouted greetings. It was our only visual contact with the rest of the fellas in the chokey.

Standing at my window, my eye was suddenly caught by something glittering deep in the exposed window reveal. The sun, directly overhead, cast its rays into the darkened gap next to the sill. Right at the bottom, a dull object sparkled at the edges.

I put my arm into the gap. Rough brickwork scratched at my skin. I hesitated slightly at the thought of monstrous spiders lurking in the depths. Gingerly, I reached down with my finger.

I touched something sharp. It moved easily, though, so the object was only small and light. With my arm in the crack, it was impossible to see what I was doing. I gripped something loosely between my thumb and second finger and slowly pulled out my arm.

I was holding the jagged end of a small bottle. The neck was long and smooth. I guessed it must have originally been a tomato-sauce bottle bought from the canteen.

The bottle ended right where the panelled sides would have been. In their place was a ragged fringe of razor-sharp glass. The whole thing was about five inches long. Held by the neck, it would be a wicked tool at close quarters. That it was in the chokey was amazing. No glass of any kind was allowed there, and someone must have smuggled it in amongst their kit. If it came to a tear-up with the screws now, at least I had a weapon.

I stared deep into the gloom of the cavity to see if there was anything else hidden there. But it was too dark to tell. There was an odd-shaped lump resting on what must have been the bottom. It could have been anything though.

Once again I put my arm deep into the cavity. My fingertips touched against something that moved. I grasped its edge and lifted. As it emerged into the daylight I was surprised to see another broken sauce bottle, identical to the first.

I put them both back where they came from. It was a good hiding place. The screws hadn't found them there. I called Joe to his window. 'Hey mate, you'll never guess what I've found.' I told him in a whisper about the bottles. 'It gives you something to think about when you come to consider all our options.'

Respecting his wish to discuss it that evening, I went and sat on my bedboard. With my back resting against the wall and my legs crossed, I closed my eyes to think.

Whatever we did, it would have to be extreme. We had been performing for months now, so it would have to be something more than just smashing up or banging all night. We could steam into a couple of the chokey screws, but that wouldn't really solve anything. We would get a VC and some more chokey.

Also it would be embarrassing. Our chokey screws were the older, more decent ones. A couple of them had gone out of their way to make things a bit easier. It would seem ungrateful, even treacherous. Especially as the real villains were the heavy mob up on the wings.

As I ran the various options through my mind, I remembered the two short bars one of the fellas had hidden in his cell. They were a pair of cast-steel hinges, which had fixed a bedboard to the wall. The bedboards were massively heavy, so the hinges had to be meaty too. Each of them was over a foot long and two inches wide. The cast steel was about half an inch thick, so there was some weight to them too.

The side walls of the cells were comparatively thin. You didn't have to be a master bricklayer to work out that they were only half a brick thick. This meant that there was barely four and a half inches of wall between Joe and me.

However, they were built of specially imported bricks, which were unbelievably hard. It was really difficult just to knock in a nail. With ordinary nails you had no chance – they would bend at the first blow. You needed special 'concrete nails'. And you had to be careful knocking these in. If you didn't hit them dead straight, they would ricochet around the cell like bullets.

So although the side walls were thin, they weren't weak. We knew that the bricks were of German manufacture. The special razor wire on the security fences was supposed to be made by them too. Trust the Germans to come up with things like these.

We were used to the massively thick walls of the old Victorian jails. The fella next door could scream his head off, and you would never hear a thing. With Albany's walls, though, if you banged on them with your fist they made a hollow, booming sound. You could hear every sound from next door. It made you feel that it wouldn't be too difficult to smash your way through. With a couple of steel bars, there just might be a chance.

Later that evening I stood at my window talking to Joe. We spoke in undertones, twisting our mouths to blur the sound and stop it carrying. We talked in slang and made oblique references to crucial items. It wasn't unknown for the screws to get up on the flat roof of the chokey and lie there listening to our conversations.

By the end of the evening we had three plans, each more extreme than the one before. We labelled them, X, Y and Z. Now, once we had explained them secretly to the other fellas, we could refer to them openly just by one of the letters.

Plan X was centred around the two steel bars. Joe agreed that it might be possible to break through the side walls with them. We could wedge our doors to prevent the screws from getting in. This would give us the time we needed.

If everyone on our side agreed, we could smash through into Paddy's, then Blackie's and then Jeff's. By then, there would be five of us. More than would normally get together in the chokey.

Just one wall would stand between us and the screws in the office. By then, though, the heavy mob would be waiting. But they wouldn't have it all their own way this time. They were all right beating people up firm handed. They'd have the riot sticks, and there would be dozens of them, but there would be five of us armed with steel bars and broken bottles.

We didn't expect to win, but it would be quite a battle. We would get a terrible beating, but we would seriously hurt a few of them too. It would be a major incident and should bring things to a head.

There would probably be a trial in an outside court too. A bit of bird on top didn't mean much when your life or your sanity was at stake. We should be able to bring out about all the beatings the heavy mob had been dishing out too.

It would certainly be a major embarrassment to the Home Office and would get us all moved. We would settle for that. Once we had done our punishment in our new jails, we'd be let up from their chokey. There would be no riot situation to justify keeping us on Rule 43.

Like Plan X, the success of Plan Y depended on a number of people joining in. In fact, the more the merrier. For a hunger-strike to succeed, you needed publicity. It was difficult to get the newspapers to publish anything about prisons anyway, what with the D-notice. Individual hunger-strikers weren't unusual. But if eight or ten of us took part, it might attract attention.

Hunger-strikes were incredibly hard though. You were in constant pain and ached all over. Weight fell off you, and you got progressively weaker. You would have no strength to fight the screws even if you wanted to. Then there was the danger of doing yourself permanent damage. There was no guarantee that it would work either. Dangerous cons starving themselves didn't excite a great deal of sympathy in most people.

As the hunger-strike went on and got progressively harder, there was always the danger that individuals might drop out. And who could blame them? Each man had his limit. It could divide us and harm our unity though. A complete failure could lead to bitterness and the end of the unified resistance.

Plan Z, as befitted its alphabetical position, was the ultimate and most extreme. It was desperation stakes, if all else failed. It was very simple and guaranteed to work. And it involved only Joe and me.

We would come out as if to go on exercise as usual. We would push Andy back in his cell and bang him up. Our chokey screws would back off as soon as they saw the broken bottles we were carrying. We would press the alarm bell and go to wait by the entrance doors. When the bullies of the heavy mob ran in, we would steam into them with the broken bottles.

It was the most desperate of tactics. We should be able to do enough damage to ensure that we were moved out, but we would get the most terrible of beatings. There would probably be charges in an outside court, but it didn't look like Joe and I were ever going to be released anyway.

It was a measure of our desperation that we should even contemplate such a plan. It was a measure of our loyalty and confidence in each other that we should undertake it together. We were men who had nothing. Our futures were bleak and barren, and filled with pain. All we had was our pride, our spirit and our honour. And, as melodramatic as it may sound to free-world people with much to live for, if you had to go down, then you might as well do so fighting the screws with your closest pal beside you.

Over the next couple of days we passed the word around about the three plans. Everyone on our side was in favour of Plan X, which was just as well if we wanted to reach the office. A couple of fellas on the other side said that they were going to try to break through their walls too. Several more said that, at the very least, they would wedge their doors.

Plan Y was even more popular. It was something anyone could take part in, wherever they were located in the chokey and whatever tools they had. It was passively non-violent. And you couldn't be nicked for it either.

Also, it was still one plan away. For the more faint-hearted it was an easy commitment. About a dozen fellas said they would take part. It was good for our unity and morale in that a large proportion of the fellas now felt that they were part of the general protest.

Plan Z met with a stony silence. You couldn't expect men with fixed sentences to get involved in something as extreme as that. Neither Joe nor I would have put anyone in a position by asking them.

No one tried to talk us out of it. Everyone knew that it was our decision. After the first mention it was never discussed again. I joked with Joe that they were either impressed by our courage or appalled by our lunacy.

Before we could put Plan X into operation we had to get the two steel bars. They were in Nuff-Nuff's cell over on Danny's side.

Nuff-Nuff was a strange fella even by Albany's standards. He was as white and as English as any of us, but he had been born in South America. By his own admission, at birth he had been an absolute monster. A cleft palate was the least of his deformities. He had been through over 20 major operations.

The finished product was far from beautiful. He was a big lad with burly shoulders, but his massive head still looked wildly out of proportion. Long, jet-black hair hung down to his shoulders. He had a bad hare-lip, which pulled his whole jaw out of shape. His speech was equally distorted.

He had a terrible complex about the way he looked. Perhaps to compensate, he always talked very loudly as if to show that he wasn't embarrassed to attract attention to himself. Consequently, his speech came out even more fractured and bizarre. At times it sounded like some large animal snuffling about. Hence the nickname, 'Nuff-Nuff', although I always called him John.

When you got to know him, though, he wasn't a bad fella. He was very lonely. He was also extremely demanding of a friendship, but if you were his pal he would do anything for you.

An out-and-out rebel, Nuff-Nuff was always rowing with the screws. This made him popular and respected amongst the fellas. It brought him more friends and acquaintances than if he had just sat in his cell quietly. Sadly, he was more at home in prison than he ever was outside.

I quite liked him, and we got on well. He wasn't short of bottle, even if he was a bit abrasive at times. Also, he tended to look up to me.

I sent a message over to him through Danny. I knew that he would have liked to use the steel bars himself, but the fellas either side of him didn't want to know. Grudgingly, he agreed that I could have them.

The bars were each wrapped in a cloth and swung from window to window until they reached Danny's cell. He brought them out on exercise, tucked down the front of his strides, hidden by his overcoat. He passed them to me as we came in. I took them into my cell with me.

At nine that evening the Night Patrol came on, and the day screws went off. We waited for ten minutes to give them time to get clear of the gate, then we started.

I had made several small wooden wedges. Using the end of the steel bar, I drove them into the gap between my cell door and the metal jamb. I spaced them out, and soon the door was wedged tight. In the background I could hear other fellas doing the same.

If the screws really wanted to get in they could do so. It would mean fetching big hydraulic jacks and would probably damage the door. But as it was late at night, with no day staff on, we figured that they would leave us till the morning. After all, we could hardly go anywhere. Or so they would think.

Standing either side of our party wall, Joe and I counted several brick courses up from the floor. Then we counted about a dozen bricks along from one end. Once we were sure that we were starting on the same brick, we began.

With a piece of rag wrapped around one end of the steel hinge, I gripped it in both hands. Standing sideways on, I swung with all my might. The end of the hinge smashed into the face of the brick, sending shock-waves right up my arms.

A dozen blows later, I stopped to survey the damage. The paint had been chipped from the surface and three-inches square of bare brick had been revealed. It was going to be a long, hard job.

I could hear the sharp cracks as Joe hit the wall from the other side. From all over the chokey came the sound of various crashes, bangs and muffled thuds. The chaps were hard at work.

All the time fellas were shouting to each other. 'Go on, Ernie, give it some stick.' 'Won't be long now, John, and I'll be through to you.' 'We're coming out, you fucking screws.' Paddy was also shouting encouragement from next door.

Much of it was bravado, designed to keep our spirits up. It was also communication. After all, we were separately locked in our own cells. If the screws came in on someone, he would warn the others.

I started back at the brick. Our plan was to knock one brick out, then it would be easier to loosen the ones around it. But it was so hard. Tiny chips of brick came away. A fine red dust hung in the air. Soon it was in my hair, coating my face and chest and drifting in an ever increasing circle.

It took all of 20 minutes before I saw daylight through the wall. Another ten saw a half-brick-sized hole gnawed through the brickword, its deep redness looking like a wound.

Joe and I both paused. It was a time to catch our breath and think about the job in hand. No one wanted to be a quitter, but it had taken half an hour to remove half a brick. At this rate it would take a dozen hours to make a sizeable hole.

Already both my hands were red raw. My eyes were streaming, and I was coughing and sneezing from the dust in my nose and mouth. My arms ached and my elbows were exquisitely sore from the constant jarring. Ignore them as I would, the doubts were there.

'Norm, hey, Norm,' I heard Joe's voice coming through the hole, 'Let me shake your hand.' Our hands met in the hole, and we symbolically shook as we laughed at the grandiose gesture.

'Oi, fellas,' I shouted at the top of my voice, 'me and Joe have just shook hands through the wall.'

There was some pride there in that we had managed to breach the wall, but it was all very tongue in cheek. It was good for morale, though, and might encourage the others. A ragged cheer went up in the chokey, followed by whistles and shouts.

'Hey, Norm, Norm.' Nuff-Nuff was yelling from the other side.

'What?' I shouted back.

'I've made a little hole, but it's impossible with what I've got.' The booming, distorted voice echoed around the chokey, giving a surreal effect to an already bizarre situation.

'It's the same with me,' bellowed Ernie from across the yard. Other voices joined in to the same effect.

'Don't worry about it, fellas,' I shouted back. 'You've done your best.'

Now it was all down to Joe and me. If it ended right here, the taste of defeat would be bitter. We wouldn't be in the best of spirits to go into a hunger-strike. Failure could effect our unity too. As isolated individuals, we would have to sit out our months in solitary.

'Norm, Norm.' It was Joe shouting through the hole again.

'Yeah?' I shouted back.

'Stand back out of the way a minute.'

I stood there puzzled. Stand back out of the way? Why? Surely I couldn't be in any danger? A locked chokey cell had to be one of the safest places on earth. What did Joe have in there, dynamite?

Suddenly, the whole cell shook. There was a deep booming sound that reverberated around the walls. I could feel the concussion through my feet as the floor shook. Then it came again.

This time, half a brick flew out of the wall, narrowly missing me. It shot across the cell and smashed heavily against the opposite wall. Small particles of brick stung my face.

I jumped back into the corner. I was shocked and puzzled. What the fuck was going on?

Bricks flew fast and furiously now. Whole bricks, half bricks and showers of fragments. Whole sections of the wall fell away. Dust was everywhere. It hung as a red mist in the air. My nose was sore from breathing it.

The booming was deafening. It was like being inside a giant drum. The back wall, against which I was leaning, shook from top to bottom. Then, as suddenly as it started, it stopped.

Voices were calling from everywhere. Ernie, John, Andy, Stan, Aussie were all shouting, wanting to know what was happening. There was concern bordering on panic. No one could conceive of anything that could have that effect in the chokey. A sledgehammer couldn't have made the deep, booming concussion.

As the dust cleared, I peered through the now gaping hole into Joe's cell. He was standing there, begrimed from head to toe. In his arms he had the bedboard, one end resting on the floor. It was incredible. He had been swinging the bedboard against the wall.

Now, a bedboard was a massive construction. There were four planks, each seven-foot long by six-inches wide, made out of inch-thick pine. An inch gap separated them. Across their back were fixed four, three-by-six-inch bracers. Massive screws held it together.

It must have weighed well over a hundredweight. It was awkward in the extreme, designed so that it couldn't be slung about. Yet Joe had been holding it in his arms and swinging it against the wall.

My own bedboard was lying on the floor, under the mattress and blankets. It was covered with a thick layer of brickdust now. I tipped the mattress and covers on to the floor and dragged the bedboard clear.

I hefted it into my arms, but its weight caused me to overbalance forwards. It was as much as I could do to hold it, let alone swing it.

I lunged towards the wall. There was little momentum, but the sheer weight caused it to smash awkwardly into the brickwork. A few bricks around the edge of the hole, already loosened, fell into Joe's cell.

Four or five times I lunged against the wall. Each time some more bricks came loose, but in nothing like the quantities that Joe had dislodged. I was no physical weakling, but I was no superman either. I stood back to let Joe continue.

Again he swung the bedboard against the wall. The bricks and mortar flew like wild, angry things. The hole yawned in the wall. It was nearly as big as a doorway now. It was large enough to step through.

Joe laid the bedboard on the floor. I climbed over two remaining courses of bricks into his cell. We slapped each other around the shoulders, laughing as tears washed tracks through the dust on our faces.

My cell was devastated. It looked like a demolition site. Brickbats lay everywhere. A thick layer of sandy, red brickdust covered everything. Joe and I were smothered from head to foot.

Joe's cell was a lot cleaner. There was a layer of dust and a few bricks close to the wall, but most of the debris had been knocked into mine. We stood at his window, breathing in lungfuls of clean, fresh air. We snorted as we tried to clear the dust from our nostrils. Our eyes burned from the irritation.

I shouted from the window that we were through the wall. I heard the insistent voice of Paddy coming from two cells along: 'Do mine next. Do mine next, fellas,' the throaty Northern Irish twang rang out.

Paddy was a young fella, who couldn't have been more than 20. He had told us he was doing a five, but he never said what for, and, of course, we never asked.

He had only been in the chokey for about a week. He had been quite restrained, but I felt that this was because he didn't know anyone. Talking to him out the window, I got the impression that he was very scatty and immature. However, he seemed to have plenty of heart.

Whether he realized the seriousness of what he got himself into was a moot point. If he had an obvious fault, it was that he would get involved in anything, no matter how crazy or bizarre. But he was old enough to make his own decisions. And as his cell stood between us and the office, we welcomed his enthusiasm.

Twenty minutes had passed, and our heads had cleared. Also, the dust had settled in my cell. Joe and I climbed through for the assault on Paddy's wall.

I pulled my bedding aside and cleared a space so that Joe had a sound footing. It was difficult enough for him to swing the bedboard without having to balance on bits of brick and other detritus. Joe picked up my bedboard and stepped up to the wall.

'Look out, Paddy, me old son,' he shouted, a smile wrinkling the corners of his mouth. Pivoting backwards and forwards like an Olympic hammer thrower, he suddenly swung the bedboard against the wall.

Once again there was a deep booming sound like the ringing of some ancient stone gong. Simultaneously, massive vibrations shook the whole cell. Joe took a couple more swings, then there was a sharp 'crack' as the brickwork ruptured. Bricks started to fall into Paddy's cell as a large hole appeared.

Within ten minutes there was an opening about three-foot square. It was big enough for us to climb through. We shouted out to the other fellas that one more wall had fallen. As they cheered we could imagine the effect on the screws.

We guessed that the day staff had been called back on duty. That in itself was a small victory. They wouldn't be pleased to be kept away from their families. It was another blow in our general campaign to remain a problem that wouldn't go away.

We also knew that, with the sort of incident into which this one was developing, the local police would have to be informed. Armed units would surround the jail in case there was an escape attempt. Footer would have a lot of explaining to do in the morning.

Joe and I scrambled through into Paddy's cell and the penultimate wall. Paddy had already cleared a space for Joe to stand in, and his bedboard was propped against the wall that adjoined

Blackie's cell. He was highly excited. It looked like he was having more fun than he'd had in a long while.

Once again I wondered if he really understood what he was getting himself into. Did he realize that what awaited us the other side of the office wall wasn't exactly a welcoming party? The night would end with blood and broken bones, most of them ours.

As we brushed aside Paddy's effusive welcome, we heard someone calling Joe's name. It was coming from outside the window, from the direction of Blackie's cell. Joe walked over to the window. I followed close behind.

It was definitely Blackie's voice, but it was low and indistinct. Joe could hear it because he was right up against the window, but I could only make out occasional words. I couldn't figure out why Blackie was whispering. Perhaps he had seen something outside his window and was warning us.

Joe turned back from the window, his face grim. He didn't say anything for several seconds. Whatever it was, it had obviously troubled him. I waited with a growing sense of impending disaster.

'Blackie doesn't want to take part,' he announced suddenly.

'What?' I said incredulously.

'Blackie says that he's thought about it, and he'd rather not take part,' Joe repeated matter of factly.

'Well, fuck him,' I said angrily, 'he should have thought of that before we started. We need to go through his cell to get to Jeff, and Jeff's all for it. Fuck him. Just smash through his wall, and if he doesn't want to get involved let him make his way down to your cell and sit there until it's all over.'

Joe looked pained. We had expended a lot of time and effort to get to our present point. We were committed now. But Joe was a man of great principle, especially where one of our own was concerned. Blackie had been involved in plenty of things in the past.

'No, Norm,' he said coming to a decision, 'he's entitled to make up his own mind. We'd be out of order to involve him against his will. This is a serious coup. People will get hurt, and there could be further charges. You and I have got nothing to lose. I'm not going to drag someone into something against their will and get them extra bird.'

As angry as I was I recognized that he had a valid argument. We thought of ourselves as honourable men, especially with regard to each other. It was the screws who were disloyal and unprincipled. If we acted likewise it would undermine our belief in ourselves.

'OK, Joe, I take your point. But all that's really happened is that his arsehole's gone,' I added vindictively.

'Even so, he's entitled to make his choice,' replied Joe patiently.

'Well, what about Jeff? Who's gonna tell him, you or me?'

'Blackie's already told him,' said Joe quietly.

We stood in silence for a minute or so. As the adrenalin rush slowed in our blood so a sense of anticlimax descended upon us. Surprisingly, the normally effervescent Paddy was silent too. As daft as he could be he realized that he had better keep his peace.

The silence hung in the air like an awkward thing. Joe and I were too close to fall out over something like this. And, anyway, we were still in a serious situation together. Unless we were going to give up and come out peacefully, at some stage the screws would have to steam in. So there could still be a battle.

'What're we going to do then, Joe?' I asked, breaking the silence.

'Let's go back to my cell and talk about it,' he replied. 'And bring your cups.'

He climbed through the hole back into my cell with me close behind. With a puzzled look on his face, Paddy picked up his plastic cup and followed. He must have thought us Englishmen very odd. So violent one minute, yet so calm and civilized the next.

The dust had completely settled in Joe's cell. Paddy and I sat down on some bedding against the unblemished end wall. Joe rummaged inside the cloth in the corner. Turning, he presented Paddy and me with a sandwich each. We had made some earlier, knowing we would need food through the night.

He took our cups and poured orange juice from a plastic bottle. He topped them up from a large white water jug. He stirred each with a spoon, then handed them to us.

This ritual was carried out in complete silence. It was strangely calming, as if it had brought order to the chaos. What could be more civilized than to sit down and eat together, in spite of the bizarre surroundings?

Paddy still hadn't said a word. Once again I couldn't help but think that he felt us English to be very strange. I could imagine him telling his mates back home about it: 'Seriously, boys, I fully expected them to get out some serviettes for us to tuck under our chins!'

For the first time now I was able to take a good look at Paddy and weigh him up. He was every bit as young as I first thought and typically Irish, with the gaunt face and high cheekbones. His jet-black hair was unfashionably short, his sideboards up around his ears. A thin chest, narrow shoulders and long arms made him seem gangling and awkward. Yet he was only of medium height. His accent was pure 'back of the throat' Northern Irish. His blue eyes sparkled with devilment, and he had a restless energy about him.

I had to give him his due. He was a young fella in a strange country, surrounded by people he didn't know. As an outsider, he must have felt that we owed him no loyalty. Yet he was willing to make a stand with us. I resolved to try to protect him from the worst of what was to come.

Joe sat down with his own sandwich and orange juice. 'Well,' he said, 'we've got a couple of options. We've already done some serious damage. This ranks as a major incident. We could say that we have made our point and come out in the morning.' He paused to chew on a mouthful of sandwich.

'Another option', he continued, 'is that, as we've got this far and are all together, perhaps we should make the most of it. We've got the iron bars. We could tell Footer that we're going to stay in here until he gives us his word that he'll do something about the screws who are giving out the kickings. If he refuses, let them come in, and we'll have a tear-up with 'em.'

Joe carried on eating, he had said his bit. 'Well, I'm in favour of the second one,' I said immediately. 'We've come this far, we might as well finish it. We expected it to end in a tear-up anyway.'

'What about you, Paddy?' asked Joe, looking towards him.

Paddy sat there, mouth full of sandwich, cup half way to his lips. Clearly he hadn't expected to be consulted.

But this was a different matter entirely to that of Blackie's involvement. Paddy was in this as much as we were. He would be punished the same as we would, and if it came to a tear-up he would get beaten up too. His opinion now carried equal weight to either of ours.

He might not have been participating in the debate, but he had been following closely. 'Let them fucking come in,' he said without any hesitation.

'Nice one, Paddy,' said Joe smiling. 'We'd better get some sleep and build up our strength. It could be a hard day tomorrow.'

I called out the window, then through the vent in the top of the door, to let the others know what we had decided. A couple said that they would stay wedged up, too, until Footer made a decision to end our confinement under Rule 43. It all added to the pressure on him.

Paddy and I fetched some blankets from our cells and made up a bed each. It would be crowded with the three of us sleeping on the floor, but we had to stay together in case the screws suddenly forced their way in during the night.

My cell was designated the khazi. We put our three piss-pots in there, together with our water jugs and washing bowls. I could hardly complain. Any further mess would be academic.

We said our goodnights and settled down to sleep. We must have been exhausted, both physically and mentally. None of us remembered falling asleep.

I came awake early the following morning, wondering where I was. I woke with a start, the legacy of the fear from the previous night. It hadn't been a relaxed sleep. The shade of Morpheus had provided only a temporary respite. I lay there contemplating the challenges of the coming day.

I was cold and stiff. As I stretched my aching limbs I saw Paddy turn restlessly and come awake too. Perhaps my moving had startled him. All of us were living on the edge. Our nerves were stretched to the limit. Even the tiniest things registered subliminally and rang warning bells.

I got up and stepped into my cell to have a piss. In the cold light of dawn the devastation seemed to stand out more starkly than it had in the half light of the evening before. If I had needed reminding, it brought back to me the extent of the damage we had done. To my good knowledge no one had ever smashed through the walls in a chokey before. If we surrendered now, it would be many a long day before Footer let me back up on the wings.

I returned to Joe's cell with a pack of sandwiches I had put aside. The outer wrappings of newspaper was thick with dust, but it hadn't found its way inside. Joe was awake now. I gave him and Paddy a sandwich each. We sat there eating, not saying a word.

We could hear the sounds of others waking in the chokey: the splash of water as someone washed in their bowl; a hawking sound as someone else spat out of a window. All the intimate sounds of men going about their ablutions. In prison, you soon learned to live without privacy.

We took it in turns to go next door and wash. We greeted each other cheerily as if to live under such conditions was admirably acceptable. Paddy even whistled and burst into snatches of song. But it was all contrived.

The cold presence of fear lurked in my stomach. Ignore it as I might, it was still there. I would never desert Joe and Paddy, but I dreamed of being a thousand miles away. Everything in my life was pressure and pain now, there wasn't one second's respite. But although I felt fear, I wasn't afraid of what was to come. I welcomed it as some deadly consummation, but let it just be over.

We heard the screws come on duty for their daytime shift. They immediately checked each cell for the morning count. I heard the screw go to Paddy's cell, then mine, before pausing to stare through the spy-hole at the three of us in Joe's cell.

Twenty minutes later we heard the breakfast trolley come around. The smell of the hot food reminded us of our hunger, in spite of the sandwich we had eaten earlier.

The screw knocked on the door and shouted through, asking whether we wanted breakfast, an obvious ploy to get us to open the door. It would take a bit more than a poxy meal to get us to come out. Three voices cried 'Fuck off' in unison.

Later, Punchy came to the door to tell us that Footer would be down to see us very shortly. 'Well, we ain't coming out. So unless he wants to talk through the door he'd better come to the window,' I shouted back. I regretted being so abrupt with him, because he had been a decent fella in the past, and I knew that the present situation bothered him. But the battle lines were clearly drawn now.

'Oi, Norman. What's happening?' Nuff-Nuff's deafening roar made us all jump. Apart from all the other problems, his volume control badly needed adjusting. He was only across the corridor, a couple of cells along.

His shout started others off. I heard Roy, a robber doing 12 years, shouting from the far end, then Ernie and Stan joined in from the other side. Smaller voices could be heard on the periphery. One of our strengths in the chokey was that we communicated well with each other. At the first sign of trouble we were all up at our windows or doors finding out what was going on.

I shouted across to Nuff-Nuff that Footer was coming down to talk, knowing that my voice would carry to most, who would pass it on to the rest. 'I'll let you know what happens,' I concluded.

Shortly afterwards I heard the gate into the exercise yard open. It was too early for exercise. I jumped up and looked out the window. Sure enough, Footer and the Chief were coming out.

'Hey, Joe, here's Footer,' I called over my shoulder.

'Yeah, well, let's not seem too keen to see him,' he replied. I stepped back from the window to stand beside him.

'I could always slip up to Paddy's cell and clump him with one of the bars as he comes past,' I said smiling.

'If things don't go right, maybe you can catch him on the way back,' answered Joe.

Suddenly, the short, fat form of Footer filled the window. One hand rested on his walking stick, in the other he held a large white handkerchief with which he mopped his large, florid face. He was perspiring heavily. Whether it was the early morning exertion or the tenseness of the situation I couldn't tell. And, in truth, I didn't care. He deserved all he got. He knew that his screws were beating people up on the wings. He could stop it if he really wanted to.

'What's this all about?' he asked, looking directly at me.

'Well, Guv ——,' began Joe, but that was as far as he got.

'I'm not speaking to you, I'm speaking to Parker,' Footer interrupted sharply.

I was astounded. I didn't think he had it in him. He knew of Joe's fearsome reputation, yet it had been a deliberate snub. Perhaps the sight of his smashed chokey cells had finally galvanized him. He continued to look at me.

'Well, Guv,' I said, deliberately using the same opening words so that he would know that we both spoke with one voice, and it didn't really matter which one of us he spoke to. 'We've made this protest because your screws continue to beat people up up on the wings. It's also about being kept down here on 43.'

He screwed up his face and continued to look at me. Coming to a decision he said, 'Parker, I won't discuss anything under these circumstances. I want you, or any other representative, to come out and discuss this in a civilized fashion in my office.'

'But what about your screws outside the door?' I countered immediately.

'They won't lay a hand on you, I give you my word.'

'And what about coming back in here afterwards?' I pressed.

'You will be allowed back in,' he assured.

'OK, Guv, we'll talk about it and let you know,' I said, trying not to sound too dismissive. It must already have been quite humiliating for him to have to come to us. Governor's call-ups usually worked the other way around. And it was all happening in front of the Chief and the assembled screws. Although we were in the driving seat now, it wouldn't always be so. I didn't want to antagonize him so much that his desire for revenge outweighed his better judgement.

Footer and the Chief walked back up the alley bounded by the breeze-block wall. I turned to Joe and Paddy. 'Well, what do you think?' I asked.

'Once you're outside that door there's no guarantee that he'll keep his word,' said Joe gravely.

'I know that, Joe, but if they do jump on me they'll know that the rest of you won't come out without a fight,' I reasoned.

Joe didn't look convinced. His experience was that logic and rationality rarely found a place in official thinking. Paddy didn't look convinced either. Irish or not, he knew he was safe in here. Outside the door there were dozens of screws with big black boots, who would love to jump all over his head. His look said that only a daft Englishman could even be thinking about it.

'I'll ask the others,' I said.

I pulled a chair up close to the door and stood on it so that my mouth was level with the ventilation holes. 'Fellas,' I shouted, 'Footer wants someone to come out and talk to him about it in his office.' There was a deathly silence.

'And who's going to do that?' asked a voice that sounded like Roy's from down the landing. It was an obvious question.

'I'll go out. But, listen, fellas. If they take any fucking liberties with me, don't come out. Make them break their way in and smash the fuckers with everything you can lay your hands on,' I shouted back defiantly. I knew the screws were outside in the corridor and could hear every word.

There was no argument or alternative suggestions. 'OK, you screws, move away from the door, and I'll come out,' I shouted again. 'Danny, let me know if they're clear.' I put my eye to the vent holes and could see that there were none opposite. Danny would do the same.

'You're OK, Norm,' came Danny's shout.

I jumped down from the chair and turned to Joe. 'Take care, mate,' I said as we shook hands.

'You take care,' he replied passionately as he grasped my hand in both of his.

'Take care, Paddy,' I said as I turned to shake hands with him too. He shook my hand vigorously but said nothing. I could see dampness in the corner of his eyes and emotion working his face. We had known each other only a short while, but there was a strong bond. We would sacrifice ourselves for each other, and there was something noble in that. I knew that, if asked, both he and Joe would willingly walk in my place.

I didn't have a lot of time to think about it, but I mused that ordinary men in the free world would rarely experience comradeship such as this. Their lives were filled with all the mundane treacheries that working men lapse into just to get by. Conformity could become, by insidious degrees, dishonourable. I would embrace my rebelliousness even if I got my head kicked in during the process.

We levered the wedges from the door jamb with the handles of our plastic knives. 'OK,' I shouted through the crack, 'someone unlock the door.'

I heard the sound of footsteps, then a key turned in the lock. The footsteps receded. With Joe and Paddy standing guard with a steel bar each, I pulled the door slightly open and peered through the crack. I could see Danny's door and the blank wall at the end of the corridor. There were no screws.

I pulled the door wider and quickly stepped outside. I heard it shut behind me and the wedges being hammered in again. I turned to look up the corridor. It was black with screws. From two doors up screws lined either side right the way up to the office.

In the open area before the office there were dozens more. Each stood stiffly to attention, eyes staring fixedly to the front. Light glistened from shiny black peaks. Serried lines of shiny black toe-caps winked from the floor. Grim, pasty white faces stared starkly from a background that was unrelievedly black.

Suddenly I felt exhilarated. The fear was driven from me in a rush of adrenalin. The sheer overkill of the intimidation had the opposite effect. There would be no shame in being overwhelmed by this multitude. If all this was for my benefit it was quite a tribute.

I walked between the sombre honour guard, an arrogant, confident mouse overshadowed by the lines of threatening cats. The whole chokey had gone deathly silent. I could imagine all the fellas listening apprehensively at their doors.

Not one screw said a word. No one made the slightest hostile gesture. Yet as I passed I felt their hatred as a physical thing. They would have loved to leap on me and batter me senseless. But they were under orders.

Coolly, calmly, looking straight ahead, I walked towards the open office door. There was no swagger. I wasn't going to take advantage of the situation. I didn't only represent myself, the fate of others depended on the outcome.

Inside the office Footer sat behind the desk, the Chief at his shoulder. I walked to stand on the plastic mat just before them. I heard someone close the door behind me.

'Well, what's the matter, Parker?' Footer requested, without any preliminaries.

'You know what's the matter, Governor,' I replied. 'Your screws up on the wings keep beating people up. Then they charge them with assault to cover themselves.'

'Which ones?' Footer asked.

I reeled off the names of the six worst culprits. 'It will only stop when you move them out. And that's what me and the fellas want,' I said.

'Give me a couple of days to look into it, but in the meantime you'll have to stop this protest.'

That was as much as I was going to get from him. 'OK, Governor, I'll go back and tell the fellas.'

I turned and headed for the door. There were two screws standing just inside. One opened it, and I walked out. All the other screws were standing just as I had left them.

I walked back down the landing. As I neared Joe's cell a single screw stepped over and put his key in the lock. 'It's OK, Joe, open the door,' I shouted out. There was the sound of wedges being removed again, the screw turned the key and walked away. The door opened, and I stepped inside.

I didn't exactly say, 'Thank fuck for that,' but I certainly felt that way. However, it was all pressure. The situation we were still in had yet to be resolved.

Joe and Paddy welcomed me back. I told them what Footer had said. He hadn't rejected our demands out of hand. He had asked for names and time to consider the situation, so it was an inquiry of sorts. And what else was there to do? Our plan to smash through the walls until we got into the office couldn't proceed now. We had no food and dire conditions. A hunger-strike would be hard enough without being wedged up three handed in a wrecked cell.

And if the screws left it for a few days then forced their way in, we'd probably be too weak to do much about it. The logical course of action was to come out and await the outcome of Footer's investigations. We could always go on to Plan Y if he reneged.

But it wasn't always down to logic. Pride and, above all, morale were important too. Every day of resistance was a personal sacrifice. It was easier to cower in your cell and retreat, but that way lay the death of the spirit. And spirit was everything.

It would have to be talked over anyway. We weren't the only ones wedged up. It would be a group decision. Perfect democracy, even though some would be swayed by others.

I pulled a chair close to the door again. I climbed up and put my mouth to the ventholes. 'Fellas,' I bellowed, 'this is what Footer said. He asked me for names. I told him the six worst, and I said they had to be moved. He said he would look into it. In the meantime he wants us to come out. What do you think?'

'What do you think?' shouted Roy. 'You're the ones in the worst trouble. They'll come in on you first.'

I turned to Joe and Paddy. 'I'll carry on, if anyone wants to carry on,' said Joe peremptorily. 'But it wasn't much use you putting yourself on offer if we aren't going to give him a chance to do something. If he fucks us about, we can still go on and do the hunger-strike.'

That was exactly my sentiments. I looked at Paddy, and he nodded in agreement. In some ways the abrupt halt at Blackie's wall had left a sour taste. We had psyched ourselves up for a big showdown. Anything else would be an anticlimax. We wouldn't be sorry to be out of this situation.

Anyway, it was hardly defeat. We had smashed through two of their special German brick walls, a victory not short on symbolism. We had kept the screws out of their beds all night.

Old Bill surrounding the nick had turned it into a major incident. And Footer's small and overstressed heart had had another couple of worry lines added to it. Any honourable settlement deserved consideration.

'Us three think we've made our point for now,' I shouted to Roy. 'And if Footer double-crosses us we'll go right ahead with Plan Y.' I thought that just about summed it up.

'That's all right by me,' shouted Roy immediately.

'And me,' grunted Nuff-Nuff. Other voices joined in in agreement.

'I'll ask Ernie, Stan and the others on the other side,' I shouted as I stepped down.

The other side agreed. Most of them had heard me anyway. I climbed back on the chair. 'Looks like we're coming out,' I yelled.

There was the sound of banging as fellas knocked their wedges out. Then it was just a matter of sitting there until the screws got around to unlocking you. I guessed they'd do us first. They would want to get the worst of the situation over with.

Sure enough, Joe's door opened, and there was Punchy. 'I hope we're going back in these cells after they've been repaired,' I said before he could start. Punchy looked anguished. He had come this far peacefully.

I suppose he figured that once the bedboards were screwed to the wall again, and we'd lost our steel bars, there would be no danger of it happening again. It wasn't much to concede. He agreed.

Our protest must have unnerved Footer, because none of us was nicked for damaging the walls. The reasoning must have been that if we performed like this in the relatively better conditions of Rule 43, what would we do on punishment? It was an admission of weakness and the first sign of concessions.

Unfortunately, it was also the last. The fat weakling had known all about the gang of screw bullies. They represented extreme opinion amongst the screws, but to discipline them would bring a screws' revolt. We were the weaker party, or so he thought. He did nothing.

A couple of days went by. We had never known the Works Department to move so fast. Usually, they were a byword for ineptitude and delay. On the third day, Joe, Paddy and I were shown back into our original cells.

We might have known that the Works hadn't performed any architectural feats. We expected bare, new brickwork and wet cement. What we didn't expect was a massive rusty steel plate bolted either side of each hole.

It was straight out of *The Works Book of Bodges*. It was both ugly and impractical. The latter because we could now hear every sound in the next cell. Paddy, Joe and I would be having some rather public bowel movements from now on.

It was also dangerous. The one, massive bolt stuck three inches clear of the plate. All the better to brain yourself if you stood up quickly.

We didn't intend to stay though. Three days had passed now, and there had been no changes. Word from up the wings was that the screw bullies were still about. Footer had double-crossed us.

That evening, as we shouted across to each other, it was agreed that we should move on to the next stage. Plan Y was imminent. It wasn't an easy commitment for anyone. Hunger-strikes were exquisitely painful. They were a severe risk to your health. How far would each man go?

Once you started you were committed. To stop would be to admit failure. Different people had different strengths. If fellas dropped out one by one, it could damage morale. And we had already failed with Plan X.

For Joe and me it was especially significant. On the other

side of Plan Y, the spectre of Plan Z loomed. We had already committed ourselves. We had meant it when we said it, knowing and accepting the implications. The 'chaps' were nothing if not men of their word. We would have to follow through.

But we had a couple of days' grace yet. It was no use our going on a hunger-strike unless it got some publicity. And the Home Office would play it down for all they were worth. They would give out a totally spurious reason for our protest and underestimate the numbers involved by a fifth.

Stan was expecting a visit in three days' time. I was going to write a letter to a newspaper, setting out our grievances and the names of the people involved in the hunger-strike. Stan would smuggle it on to the visit and slip it to his visitor. The visitor would hand it in to the London offices of a national newspaper. Then the Home Office would be under pressure from within and without.

In the meantime we had three days to play with. We weren't exactly in a festive mood, but perhaps the thought of the pain and discomfort that was to come made us thankful for this brief period of respite.

That night all of us whose cells faced on to the yard were at our windows. It was warmish, with hardly a breath of air. In the velvety black sky above myriad stars twinkled in perfect focus. The bright moonlight lit the yard with an unearthly glow. It was an idyllic, almost enchanted setting. As a Hollywood film set it would have smacked of cliché.

We played Twenty Questions and other guessing games, shouting backwards and forwards across the yard. Paddy joined in enthusiastically. He had fully found his feet now. His recent involvement in the 'wall' protest had increased his standing amongst the fellas. As far as anyone was concerned, he was one of us now.

In some ways this was a double-edged weapon. Paddy was a natural extrovert. He was a talented singer, mimic and teller of jokes. His effervescent personality coupled with his boundless enthusiasm rapidly turned the proceedings into 'Paddy's Chokey Show'.

He was funny, though, and diverted our attention from darker thoughts. If he was a bit over the top, then we could tolerate that. Different people handled chokey in different ways. The important thing was that, should there be any trouble, Paddy had already proved he would stand with us. Virtually everything else was insignificant.

A couple of hours passed. Interest in the guessing games waned. There were extended lulls in the conversation. Sometimes we would go for ten minutes, just standing there in the silence, soaking up tranquillity.

Suddenly, Paddy started to sing. His high, sweet voice arose out of nowhere. It carried clearly right across the yard. He was singing 'Kevin Barry', that Republican anthem so rich in pathos. It was early days for the IRA in England, they were still a comparatively minor irritant. All politics apart, we were enchanted by the beauty of the performance.

I had the strange feeling that I was sharing a memorable experience. Amongst all the pain of solitary confinement, in a bleak and unhappy place such as the chokey, it was a magic moment. It struck a chord in me that would resonate down the years. An exquisitely beautiful experience made all the more so by the squalor of the surroundings. The only tragedy was that it would soon pass, leaving no trace for posterity.

Paddy finished the song. No one spoke. It seemed a sacrilege to break the silence, as if it would somehow break the spell. Taking his cue, Paddy launched into another one. This time it was a rousing rebel song.

It was great entertainment. Paddy was as good as any professional I'd ever heard. With no amplification or musical backing, he held us spellbound. When he was done we all said our goodnights quietly and went to bed. It was a fitting end to an evening. Anything else would have been a gross anticlimax.

Over the next couple of days I was exposed to Paddy's complete repertoire. On Blackie's side there was a brick wall: between Paddy and I a pair of massive metal plates, which acted like sounding-boards. I was the more accessible audience.

No TV watcher myself, I was soon familiar with all the jingles. According to the others, Paddy's mimicry was masterful. He had them spot on. I couldn't have told the difference.

There was one particular jingle that soon burned in my brain like a raw nerve. It was a biscuit advert that, on TV, must have been preceded by drums and the deep, deep voice of a Red Indian.

I would be laying on my bed, dozing lightly, a common enough state in the chokey. My face barely inches from the metal plate. Suddenly there would be a deep roll of Indian war-drums as Paddy beat on the plate with his knuckles.

In the background could be heard the chant of the Braves, 'Umba, daba, umba daba, umba daba, umba daba.' Finally, Sitting Bull himself would cut in. In a deeply resonant and sepulchral tone he would intone, 'Who put the figs in the Fig Rolls?'

Now it was all very funny stuff – the first time. It was brilliant mimicry, but it frightened me. (When your nerves were stretched as tight as mine you didn't need to be awakened by the disembodied voice of Sitting Bull.) After about a dozen times, though, it began to pall on me. Soon, I could cheerfully have strangled him.

On another occasion I was sitting reading when a very cultured, upper-class English voice rang out next door. It was answered by the typically sing-song voice of the Indian subcontinent. The throaty tones of a Northern Irish voice joined in, closely followed by the higher-pitched Dublin accent.

Suddenly, the broken diction of pure Cockney cut across the babble, 'Cor, fuck me. All these poxy foreigners in 'ere. All we need now is a fuckin' Yank.' Immediately, the deep, rolling tones of the Marlboro advert answered, 'Say, did somebody call my name?'

It was hilarious. It actually sounded like there were several different nationalities in the cell next door. I had a professional entertainer for a neighbour.

Unfortunately, I wasn't always in the mood. Often, he would bring me back from some deep reverie where I was lost to the world. Once again, the harsh realities of the chokey would flood in. My only consolation was that the pain and discomfort of the impending hunger-strike would slow him down a bit. Even Paddy would find it difficult to sing and joke when he was starving to death.

Stan duly had his visit, and the letter was smuggled out. The following morning ten of us refused breakfast. The screw looked at me quizzically when I told him I was on hunger-strike. 'I've still got to put your meal in,' he said. I knew that was part of the rules. I stepped back, and he put the metal tray on the floor. Plan Y was under way.

Even though it was the first meal I would miss, I realized I would soon feel the effects. I was so used to being fed at specific times, day in, day out, that if a meal were to be delayed by only half an hour my stomach would quickly feel hunger pains.

I started as I intended to carry on. I picked up the tray and pissed on the porridge and bread and jam. However long the tray stood in the corner now, I wouldn't be tempted to eat from it.

By mid-morning the hunger was a gnawing pain in my stomach. I went on exercise with Joe and Danny as usual but felt cold. Without food for fuel the body couldn't keep warm. We walked and talked of anything except food and the nascent hunger pains. I was pleased to come in, but even back in the cell I couldn't get warm.

Dinner-time arrived, but instead of being a welcome break in the monotony it was a time of trial. Never had the bland prison food looked so appetizing. The screw took the piss-soaked breakfast tray out, wrinkling his nose as he did so. The pungent urine smell wafted across to me. I could do without living with that in my nostrils all the time. I resolved not to foul the meals again. Will-power would have to be enough.

Received wisdom had it that if you drank plenty of water it allayed the worst of the hunger pangs. I drank it by the pint, but in my chilled condition all it served to do was to make me piss constantly.

Tea-time came and went. The meal sat in the corner to tempt me through the night. As I lay on my bed trying to read, the insidious food smells titillated my nostrils. I told myself that if I had just the tiniest taste, that brief satisfaction would be enough. But I knew that it would only make it worse.

That evening we talked out of our windows as usual, but our hearts weren't in it. It was cold standing there in the night air and the hunger pangs were so fierce that I felt sick.

To add to my discomfort, a mild headache started. It registered almost subliminally, only occasionally forcing its way into consciousness. But I was aware that it was there.

Hunger kept me from sleep. I couldn't keep my mind from the pangs. My body seemed to ache in several different places simultaneously. Only by screwing myself tightly into a foetal position beneath the covers could I temporarily escape it. Eventually, in the early hours of the morning, sleep born of exhaustion overtook me.

I woke the following day and was immediately aware of the low-level ache that suffused my whole being. If I had thought that the pangs would be restricted to my stomach then I was sorely mistaken. There was an aching, yawning chasm in my gut, but that vied for attention along with my headache and a bone-deep chill.

I felt listless as I walked on exercise. I realized that, within days, strenuous physical activity would be out. It wouldn't be too long before even walking was beyond me.

Contact between us had dropped to a minimum now. No

one seemed to have the enthusiasm to start a conversation. Thankfully, Sammy Davis Jnr next door was also suffering. There were no songs, no impersonations and no Red Indians selling Fig Rolls.

As the third day dawned on our misery, I found that the hunger pains had abated somewhat. Someone had once told me that the first three days were the worst. After that the pangs died away. Well, they certainly hadn't died away yet, but they had become more of a dull ache throughout my body.

As time passed, Punchy had been looking increasingly strained. His face was white and drawn as he supervised the delivery of the meals. He had been on duty every day since the latest trouble began. Perhaps he was refusing leave until the problem was resolved.

Late on the afternoon of the third day my door opened suddenly, and Punchy hurried in. 'Look, Parker,' he said, 'I've seen the Governor and told him that if he doesn't do something shortly, I and my staff will refuse to man the block. I told him that, so far, your protests have been passive and not aimed at us. But that soon you would have no alternative but to turn on us. He has told me that if you stop your hunger-strike you will all be moved. Either you or Joe will go tomorrow; the other one two days later and the rest of you after a week. Just as soon as arrangements can be made. He's given me his word on this, and I give you my word on it too.'

From the look on his face you would have thought that it was Punchy who was under all the pressure. But he was a caring man and couldn't conceal a grudging respect for us. Also, he wasn't a bad judge of men. He knew that we were determined not to give in. He realized that we were running out of options. Our protests were becoming increasingly desperate.

It sounded like an attractive solution and about the best we were going to get. Especially for Joe and me. But we were in this with the rest. Joe and I might be moved, then no one else. They would think that they had got rid of the ringleaders and that the protests would end. The rest might be left there for months. 'I'll have to talk to the others, Guv,' I said. 'We've discussed everything else between us.'

'That's OK,' said Punchy, 'I'm going around to everyone personally so you all know exactly what's happening.'

He went out. Seconds later I heard him open Joe's door. I waited for him to finish and come out again. I called Joe to his window. 'Well, what do you think?' I asked.

'If they keep their word it's a victory of sorts,' Joe replied.

I called through the doorvents to Roy, Nuff-Nuff, Danny and the others opposite. They were all of the same opinion as Joe.

'I ain't worried about changing the jail,' I shouted. 'I'm not fighting for all those fuckers up on the wings who haven't got the arsehole to stand up for themselves. I'm only concerned about us. We're the ones in the chokey.'

The fellas shouted their agreement and said that they were willing to take the chance that they would be moved.

Joe and I then called over to Ernie, Stan and Jim and the rest on the other side of the yard. They were unanimously for the plan. I rang my bell, and Punchy came and opened my door.

'So, we've all agreed to stop the hunger-strike. But if Footer double-crosses us again and goes back on his word, then the fellas that remain here won't stop tearing up,' I finished defiantly. I regretted it as I said it. The threat brought an almost imperceptible hurt look to Punchy's face. He was a proud man who had gone out of his way to behave decently. 'By the way, Guv, the fellas appreciate what you've done for us,' I added quickly.

Punchy acknowledged the concession and implied apology. 'OK, Parker,' he said, 'I wish it hadn't come to all this.' He turned and left.

That night we were all up at our windows. There was almost a holiday mood, brought on by thoughts of our imminent departures. On my part the euphoria was genuine, because, as one of the first two to go, I was confident that I would get out. Apart from Joe, the others must have had their doubts. But they were putting on a brave face about it.

Paddy was in fine form. He sang all his most rousing rebel songs, told dozens of jokes and did impersonation after impersonation. My spirits rose even further at the thought that, very shortly, I would never have to listen to the Fig Roll Indian again. It was all forgiven now though.

Joe and I talked late into the night. In one way it was a sad time for us, because it was a parting of close friends. For years we had kept in touch through messages carried by mutual friends. And, finally, when we had got together in the same jail, it had to be Albany in the middle of a riot.

Joe and I inhabited a strange world. We were men who carried all our emotional baggage with us. The outside world was a far and distant place. Seeing our families once a month for a two-hour visit only served to increase our sense of isolation and loneliness. Our souls were sustained by just a few strong bonds of friendship.

But we were warriors in a harsh gladiatorial school. The most crucial requirement was strength, in all its forms. Strength to survive the physical rigours of solitary confinement, beatings and bread and water. Strength to survive the emotional vacuum in which we existed. We were spiritual sailors, for ever condemned to sail the seas with no port to call home. In the final analysis we were lonely, lonely men. For Joe and I there would be sadness in our parting.

I woke early and lay there in the darkness. Instead of the usual pain and despair, there was hope in my heart. I savoured the thought that even if I didn't go today then Joe would. But I had a strange feeling that it would be me.

I heard the screws come on duty. I felt my heart quicken. The breakfast trolley came around. Just before my door closed Punchy told me that I would be moving right after breakfast.

Suddenly my problems were over. Wherever I was going I

wouldn't be on subversive 43. I was embarking on a whole new adventure. The only news that could have cheered me more was that I was to be released.

I went to my window and called for Joe. I told him I was going, and he was genuinely pleased for me. 'Take care, Norm, I don't think I'll be far behind you,' he said. 'I'll drop you a card when I get settled.' It was an emotional moment. There was nothing else to say.

My door opened, and there stood two screws I hadn't seen at Albany before. I guessed they were part of the escort from another jail. I picked up my few belongings and walked out after them.

I went to Joe's door. I banged twice with my fist. 'I'm off, Joe,' I shouted. I turned away quickly as he called his muffled reply. 'Danny, John, Roy, Jeff,' I shouted as I passed along the corridor, 'You all take care. And, don't forget, NO FUCKING SURRENDER.' Several voices called out in reply.

As I reached the gate leading to the yard, I called to Ernie, Stan and Jim down the other corridor. With their farewells ringing in my ears I walked out into the yard, the two screws beside me.

The open sky and fresh air were invigorating. I breathed deeply, and my heart filled with hope for the future. I walked away from a part of my life that I would never see again. By comparison, the future looked rosy.

Two days later, as promised, Joe was moved to Wandsworth. A week later Roy followed him. Over the next month several others went too. However, that was the lot. Footer double-crossed us in the end. The half dozen that remained were kept in the chokey for over a year before they were moved. One of them, Jim, was to be shot dead by armed police, several years later, rather than come back to prison.

14. Of Escapes, Principles and Prison Politics

O f all the Albany rioters, I had come out of the situation the best. Whereas others had gone to tightly run local prisons or long-term jails that were experiencing their own problems, I went to the Scrubs.

In many ways Wormwood Scrubs was a strange jail. Firstly, it served a multitude of penological uses. 'A' wing alone housed three distinct categories of prisoner. There were those who had come from all over the country to await operations in the prison hospital. Then there were those awaiting allocation to other prisons. Finally, in an area partitioned off from the rest of the wing, there was the Segregation Unit. This contained men doing punishment for infractions of prison rules.

'B' wing was the boys' wing. Here, prisoners under 21 awaited transfer to various Young Offender institutions. The wing was notoriously volatile. Apart from all the mischief that 300 teenage boys could cause during the day when they were unlocked, the nights were literally bedlam. Many stood at their windows until daybreak, singing, calling out messages and shouting abuse at each other.

'C' wing, also notoriously volatile, housed both remands and those awaiting allocation. With men kept three to a cell, there could often be upwards of 500 prisoners on the wing. The remands would be ferried backwards and forwards to court on a daily basis. Those awaiting allocation ranged from men doing nine months to those doing life. The short termers would go to jails all over the country; the lucky amongst the long termers would get a place in 'D' wing, after spending several months on a waiting list.

'D' wing was the long-term wing. It housed over 300 men doing from five years to life. The prisoners were, in the main, carefully screened and selected. Many were 'stars', who had never been in prison before. The rest were mostly well-behaved, model prisoners. There was rarely any trouble. Apart from the fact that the cons were carefully selected, there were many benefits from being on 'D' wing.

Firstly, the wing was very relaxed and easygoing. You were unlocked from 7.30 a.m. until 9.00 p.m. and enjoyed a range of facilities and privileges that were the envy of many long-term jails. Perhaps the greatest benefit, though, was that the Scrubs was in the heart of London. This meant that Londoners could get their visits easily and generally keep in touch. Lastly, the parole rate was quite good on 'D' wing.

I had noticed on my travels through the system that the authorities allowed these pockets of relatively civilized conditions to exist. It wasn't done for humanitarian reasons, but rather to encourage and control. At the first sign of trouble on 'D' wing, the perpetrator would be immediately shanghaied. He might spend a short time in the Segregation Unit beforehand, but, ultimately, he would be transferred to another, much worse, jail.

In the light of all this it might seem strange that the authorities had seen fit to send me to the Scrubs from the riot-torn Albany. Perhaps they didn't intend for me to go to 'D' wing. Most likely the right hand didn't know what the left one was doing, as usual. However, there was an unofficial policy whereby a particularly troublesome prisoner was put in amongst a well-behaved prisoner population. The logic was threefold. The troublemaker would discover it difficult to find other, like-minded cons; he just might learn to enjoy the good facilities and fear to lose them and, lastly, some of the good behaviour of the vast majority might just rub off on him. Ergo, my transfer.

I duly arrived in Scrubs reception, still on the 'A' list; in 'patches' from my Albany escape attempt; half-starved from the hunger-strike and with a disciplinary record that could hardly have been worse.

There was an immediate problem. 'C' wing's Governor refused to have me on his already volatile wing. This left only two options: the Seg. or 'D' wing. Now, comparatively speaking, the Scrubs' Segregation Unit was a decidedly lightweight operation. It served a convict population that was relatively well behaved, with particularly troublesome prisoners being transferred out. The chokey screws didn't have regularly to restrain and control men over periods of time. There was little brutality.

It didn't make much sense to put me in there. If I had proved too much for Albany's extremely robust chokey, I wouldn't last five minutes in Scrubs Seg. So it was to be 'D' wing.

There was another immediate problem. Although 'D' wing housed men on the 'A' list, it didn't accept those in 'patches'. So, in the continuing spirit of conciliation and accommodation, I was taken out of 'patches' and moved over to 'D' wing.

Now even on the well-behaved 'D' wing, there was a small group who were to be considered the 'chaps', both by others, as well as by themselves.

As in every other jail, membership of this elite club was largely self-proposed. Fellas nominated themselves by their deeds or their attitude. Acceptance was solely determined by whether or not the rest of the 'chaps' acknowledged you. Objective criteria were arcane and obscure, but, generally speaking, if most 'chaps' in good standing considered you to be a tosser or a slag, it was either social ostracism or the river. There were, however, occasional, isolated, wannabee-chaps who belonged to an exclusive club of one.

This all gave rise to an extremely high level of gossip, intrigue and general backbiting. Any macho, sexist notions I ever had that gossiping and backbiting were purely the preserve of women were soon dispelled after a few years in prison. Of all the mental pressures, 'prison politics' rates amongst the highest.

Luckily for me, though, being accepted was one problem I definitely didn't have. I was doing life for my second, 'gangland' killing; I had been in riots, escapes and hunger-strikes; I was partially deranged because of a depressive mental illness, and I was violent on a regular basis to any one at all who upset me. I wasn't the ultimate 'chap', but if there had ever been elections to a national committee, I could probably have got myself nominated.

I didn't get a standing ovation or a ticker-tape parade along the 'ones', but small groups of London 'chaps' wandered over to welcome me. Some I knew personally, others were friends of friends.

I soon learned that one of the most valued privileges at the Scrubs was to 'dine out', if you wanted to. This meant that you could eat your meals at communal tables placed crosswise along the length of the 'ones'. About three-quarters of 'D'-wing cons took advantage of this privilege. There were about 20 tables. I soon found out that the elite amongst the Scrubs 'chaps' dined out on tables 4 and 13.

To the uninitiated, it might have seemed that table 4 seated the cream of the cream. Freddie, of the Kray gang, was capable, influential and well respected. Three of the 'Great Train Robbers', Gordon, Jim and Buster, were there largely by virtue of the respect their crime had attracted. Frank and George were two experienced North London bank robbers. Then there were a couple of young, wannabee 'chaps', who basked in the reflected glory.

As the leading lights of table 4 were mostly middle aged and well behaved, they were looked on by everyone as a calming influence. This could hardly be said of table 13, where the other concentration of the 'chaps' dined out.

Billy G had recently arrived from a dirty protest at Parkhurst. A strong, honourable and determined man, the authorities feared him the most.

Alan had been in the Parkhurst riot and had been severely beaten by the screws. Now that an action for damages was pending, he had been transferred to the Scrubs to keep him quiet.

Jim and Pat were both prolific armed robbers whose cases had attracted widespread publicity. Tommy, also an armed robber, was one of seven brothers in a large, North London crime family. Martin, barely 21, had been family friend of Ron and Reg and a junior member of 'the Firm'.

Apart from Billy G, all of table 13 were quite young. Together with Billy G, they shared his volatility and hatred of the screws. They obviously thought me to be a kindred spirit. I was invited to join them on table 13.

For myself, I was quite relieved to be in a cushy jail for a change. The protests, solitary confinement and hunger-strikes at Albany had taken it out of me. I felt I could do with a period of relative peace to regroup and gather my strength. My first priority was still to escape, but it didn't have to be right away. In the meantime I could re-establish contact with my family and friends through visits.

One of the positive aspects of being moved from jail to jail was that it gave you a comprehensive frame of reference, allowing you to compare levels of security. Escape from the purpose-built, long-term jails was very difficult because you were confronted by every security measure possible. However, in the older prisons many of the security measures had been grafted on, so there were occasional gaps or shortcomings.

I quite enjoyed weighing up a new jail. Glaring weaknesses

were very few and far between, one had to look deeper. With a combination of De Bono's 'lateral thinking' and my own home-spun philosophy, I usually managed to find some chink in the armour though.

In security terms the Scrubs was trying hard to come to terms with the new breed of resourceful and desperate criminal. These were prisoners who had both a very long sentence, one from which they might never get out, and a large accumulation of wealth. For them, escape was virtually the only option. Or so you would think. In reality it was amazing how few actually gave serious consideration to it.

For many, the trauma of the trial and the subsequent long sentence had knocked the fight out of them. For others, once they had settled into a relatively cushy prison regime, they switched off. The weren't living, by any stretch of the imagination. Just existing at a very basic level. And once they had got into this rut, it was very difficult to get out of it. Apart from anything else, they just couldn't bring themselves to face the rigours of solitary confinement, bread-and-water diets and the other sanctions that went with a failed escape. Further, it takes a bit of bottle to try to escape, and they just didn't have it any more.

For myself, I had several advantages. I had grown up in and around West London, so I knew the area around the Scrubs very well. I actually went to school only a hundred yards away. I knew the layout of the inside of the prison well, because I had served an earlier sentence there, in 'A', 'C' and 'D' wings. I could call on help from many of the 'chaps' in 'D' wing. I could also call on help from friends outside in the form of having a getaway car left outside on the day of the escape. With these advantages in mind, I felt quite confident.

The major obstacle to escape from the Scrubs, and most other security jails for that matter, was a 20-foot-high wire fence that ran all around the perimeter. It stood about 16 feet inside the outer, perimeter wall and was festooned with rolls of razor-sharp barbed wire. Trembler-bells were fixed to the wire fence panels at regular intervals, so that any movement would set off an alarm. The whole of the outer perimeter was scanned by closed-circuit TV cameras. At night, powerful lights on high poles provided an illumination that was brighter than daylight.

At strategic points around the jail were positioned observation posts, which were constantly manned. Screws with dogs criss-crossed on permanent patrol. Thus far the Scrubs was as secure as any jail I had seen.

However, there were a couple of weaknesses, one of which immediately excited me. The outer perimeter wall was a massive stone construction. To its top had been fixed a large, plastic canopy, like an inverted gutter. This was to prevent a rope and hook finding purchase. But the wall wasn't very high, only about 16 feet. In the corner, where two walls met by 'D' wing, it stood only 14-foot high. Further, a camera had been fixed on top of the wall, its thick, black, plastic cable hanging down inside. This meant that anyone who could get beyond the wire fence would only have to raise themselves about 12 feet off the ground to be able to grab the plastic cable. This was a major flaw in the outside perimeter.

The other, more general weakness was that major repair work was always going on, as the Scrubs was such an old jail. This meant that there was a vast stock of tools, ladders, building materials and so on. None of this was left lying about, by any means. However, it did raise possibilities.

I was put to work in the laundry, part of an old, ramshackle, brick-built complex that stood in the yard between 'C' and 'D' wings. Most of the complement of tables 4 and 13 worked in there too, so I realized that it must be a comparatively good number.

Next door to the laundry was a paint shop. It was shared by cons on a painting and decorating course and the Works Painters

Department. There were several ladders in there. By day they were supervised by four Works' screws. By night they were chained and padlocked to a wall inside the barred and gated shop.

On close inspection of the inside of the laundry, I could see that the paint shop and the laundry had originally been one building. A partition wall had been built to separate them. The partition was plasterboard fixed to wooden framing. However, I suspected that there might be some hidden steel reinforcing. I would never be able to tell until I smashed through the plasterboard though. So I would need a pair of bolt-croppers, just in case.

Suddenly, I had the basic kernel of my plan. If I could get into the laundry outside working hours, I could then break my way into the paint shop and get at the ladders. A hammer was all I would need to knock the padlocks from the securing chains. Then I could drag the ladders through into the laundry and on to the fence. But how was I to get into the laundry?

My cell overlooked one side of the laundry and, specifically, the gate through which we would enter. Long hours of observation confirmed that the gate was never locked on the 'double'. It was single locked, of course, and a padlock was fastened through a hasp. However, the Security PO on his rounds never locked the gate with his 'doubles' key.

I always took particular interest in the movements of the Security PO in whichever jail I was in. Most strategic gates were 'doubled', but they always had to leave a few that were in constant use. From my seat at table 13 I noticed that they didn't 'double' the gate at the far end of 'D' wing until quite late in the evening. Works' screws with small parties of cons would often leave by this gate. An added bonus was that this gate wasn't under direct supervision all the time. It was partly obscured by a large TV set on a stand. Admittedly, there were often upwards of a hundred cons watching the TV, but they were so intent on what was on the screen that they hardly looked at movements through the gate.

My plan was beginning to fall into shape. Possession of a single key would allow me to slip out the end gate of 'D' wing. The outside end of the wing wasn't covered by the cameras, neither was the small yard between 'D' wing and the laundry gate through which I intended to enter. I could knock the padlock off, unlock the gate, break through the partition, drag two ladders – one large, one small – through into the laundry, exit through the gate I had entered and take a run at the fence. Provided I didn't run smack bang into a dog patrol, I could be up and over the inside fence before the screws could get to me.

One thing was immediately apparent. Apart from a gate key and several other necessary items, I would need at least one fellow escapee. He would carry the second ladder.

This proved to be a major problem. I needed someone who was brave, sensible and physically fit. Brave, to face the prospect of clambering over high, barbed-wire strewn fences and walls; of being savaged by guard dogs, shot at by armed-police response units outside and beaten up by screws if we failed. Sensible, in that they wouldn't let anyone know by words or deed what we intended to do. Physically fit, to do all the carrying and climbing.

These stringent criteria narrowed it right down. There were very few who fitted the bill. And those who did fit didn't want to go, either because they had settled into their sentence or had done long enough to get to a lower-security establishment, where escape would be much easier.

Fortunately, a partner wasn't that immediate a problem. I had many other things to do that would take weeks if not months. I would just carry on and hope that I would either find the right person or they would arrive from another jail.

I set about trying to get a singles gate key. Every screw had one, as did Works' screws, probation staff, chaplains, nurses and teachers. All had to move freely around the prison to go about their daily tasks. I wouldn't try to steal an actual key. They all had to be checked and handed in at night, and a missing key would spark off a full alert. They would change every lock in the jail that the key fitted, so it would be of no use to me anyway.

But if I could get an impression of a key, then smuggle it out, have a key made and smuggle it back again, that key would get me through any undoubled gate in the jail.

In the sex-starved world of prisons, romance is always in the air. Mostly it is imagined. Attractive and not so attractive female nurses, teachers and probation staff fuel the fantasies of many a frustrated con. Occasionally, the attraction is mutual.

It just so happened that one of the young, wannabee-chaps on the fringes of our table-13 group was having an affair with a teacher. She was a young, blonde girl, who most of us had never seen because she didn't leave the education block. The relationship had progressed through secret glances, whispers and clandestine touching, to full-blown sex in a book cupboard. Needless to say, Jimmy, our young Lothario, saw fit to share every intimate detail with his circle of friends.

I wasn't particularly interested. My old-fashioned values caused me to baulk at the idea of Jimmy betraying a trust so flagrantly. If I had harboured any further doubts that he was exploiting the woman, these disappeared when it came out that he was getting her to fetch things in. First it was just tobacco, then it progressed to bottles of drink. Experience told me that it wasn't going to last very long.

I would never have asked her myself, but the prospect of spending the rest of my life in prison concentrated my mind wonderfully. Through an intermediary, I asked Jimmy to get an impression of a key from her. Ever keen to ingratiate himself with the 'chaps', Jimmy obliged. She brought in a small piece of cuttlefish, pressed several indents of her gate key into it and handed it to Jimmy.

Now I had my impression, all that remained was to get it out. I bought a large, soft-toy teddy bear from one of 'D' wing's hobbies enthusiasts and hid the cuttlefish inside. The toy was handed out on a visit and passed to an expert key-maker friend of mine.

Whilst I awaited the return of the finished key, I set about finding the rest of the things I would need. At least one of us would have to look like a screw as we walked out of the gate at the end of 'D' wing. Luckily, this was only a minor problem. We washed all the Works screws' overalls in the laundry. There were dozens of sets of the brownish boiler suits, and there was little check kept on them. It would be easy to put a set in my personal laundry and carry it over to the wing when required.

The cap would be slightly more difficult. If a screw's cap went missing, there would be a full-scale search of the whole jail. For someone to keep it could only mean that they wanted to impersonate a screw.

Caps did go missing on a regular basis, however. Often, when the screws ran to answer an alarm bell, their hats would fall off. Mischievious cons sometimes took them and ripped them to pieces. The remains could be found in the recess or strewn about the yard. Occasionally the cap badge would be kept as a souvenir and hidden.

Not much went on in the jail that our group didn't get to hear about. It just so happened that a friend of ours on 'C' wing had ripped a cap apart a few days previously and hidden the badge. He sent it over to us, and I hid it in the laundry. Just to be on the safe side, I asked him to get another one. Within a week he had obliged.

Now I had the badges, the actual caps would be no problem. We had access to cardboard, black material and plastic, so one of the hobbies enthusiasts could soon make a couple up for us.

As for the rest of the uniform, we could get screw's shirts from the laundry and the black boots we wore differed little from theirs. I was confident I could now deck at least two of us out as passable imitations of Works' screws.

Going through my plan step by step, the next requirement

was a hammer to knock the padlock from the laundry gate. There was a small toolkit kept in the wing office for minor emergency repairs. If some con wanted to knock in a nail, or hang a poster in his cell, he could always borrow the hammer. It had to be returned by nine o'clock bang-up, but by then it would all be over for my escape anyway.

The bolt-croppers for any hidden reinforcing in the laundry partition were a big problem. They were so obviously a major escape aid that they were carefully supervised. However, we did have several pals on the Works. One of them was actually based in the laundry. There was a small storeroom he and his Works' screw used as an office and tearoom. In the corner was a cabinet containing tools. Not a pair of bolt-croppers, unfortunately, but our pal said that he used them regularly and could leave a pair in the cabinet overnight. It would bring him some heat after the escape, but they had been left there before.

There was no doubt that my faith in human nature had been damaged by the selfishness and cruelty I had witnessed in jail. In extreme circumstances the ruling creed was often 'Every man for himself'. However, there was always a small group of men who were loyal and honourable; who would sacrifice themselves for others with little thought for their own welfare. In helping me with my escape, men who hardly knew me put themselves at considerable risk, and for no reward other than my heartfelt thanks. One could only feel humble at such times.

From a material, logistical point of view, I was now ready to make my escape. The key was finished outside and could be brought in at a few days' notice. Everything else was in position. But I still didn't have a partner. No one had arrived, and, search as I might, I couldn't find anyone suitable and willing on 'D' wing. Suddenly, though, it all became academic.

One morning, as we crossed the yard for work in the laundry, I noticed a large lorry filled with scaffolding parked next to the wing. Several civilian contractors stood about under the watchful eye of a screw. As we returned from work at dinner-time, partially erected scaffolding skirted the base of 'D' wing. From friends on the Works I found out that the roof and the whole of the outside of the wing were to be renovated. The work would take several months.

At first I thought this might be a boon. The scaffolding, boards and ladders were all ideally suited for an escape. I just might find an opportunity. The reality, though, was that the scaffolding brought new and vastly increased security around 'D' wing. Special observation boxes were set up, more lights erected and patrols increased. Any hope of escape was gone until the work was over.

Several months passed, long frustrating months. There was always the possibility that some trouble would arise in which I might get involved. I had been shanghaied before. It could easily happen again. Time really was of the essence.

On the positive side, though, I had now found a partner. In fact I had found three. Ian Down was a young North London robber, doing 25 years for a string of bank robberies in Scotland. He was part Scots himself and filled with the Celtic warrior spirit. Just a few years into his sentence, he had already been involved in several tear-ups and escape attempts. We were made for each other.

Ian was instantly enthusiastic about the escape. He came to work in the laundry, so he could clearly see the full extent of the plan. Then he settled down with me to await the removal of the scaffolding.

With two of us involved, there were now two opinions. Ian pointed out that, provided we could find suitable people, four would be an ideal number for the escape. A Works' party comprising a screw and three cons would be quite normal, leaving the wing after tea. Even if it were seen crossing the yard and entering the laundry, it would excite no interest. More importantly, though, when we ran at the fence, Ian and I could carry the ladders whilst the other two could mind us off against any screws we might bump into.

Admittedly, those carrying the ladders would be first up the fence and have the best chance of getting away. However, it was quite a touch to be put into someone else's escape. And if we didn't bump into a patrol right away, there was a good chance we would all get out.

Although we had many things in common, Ian and I had quite different personalities. I burned with far more bitterness and anger than him. I was hostile and stand-offish; he was outgoing and friendly. There was no problem. Ian's way worked for him; my way worked for me. We were both surviving, when others all around us were going under.

Malcolm was one of Ian's circle of friends. His youth, clean-cut looks, good manners and intelligence made him seem out of place in prison. However, the placid exterior belied a fiery nature. He was courageous, brave and extremely determined. He was also a libertarian.

I thought I was well informed about all the various political creeds, but this was a new one on me. It turned out that Malcolm was somewhere to the left of the revolutionary Marxists. This hardly sat well with my own right-wing views, but, as Ian pointed out, we were only going to escape together, not run for office.

Apparently Malcolm had fire-bombed his local, Tory-run town hall; this kind of direct action was virtually unknown in the early Seventies. Political terrorism was still largely in its infancy. He had carried on his protests in prison and had spent months in solitary. He had lost most of the remission on his ten-year sentence. His aggression, though, was directed only at authority. I found him to be extremely pleasant and friendly. We got on immediately.

In many ways Gerry Kelley was quite similar to Malcolm.

Tall and slim, with long black curly hair that framed a pasty, baby-face, he looked more like a college student than the leader of the IRA team, who had bombed the Old Bailey a couple of years earlier.

Terrorism didn't sit easily with the 'chaps'. Many were working-class 'Little Englanders' and quite conservative in their outlook. So, whilst nonces, grasses and slags were clearly beyond the pale, terrorists occupied a grey area. However, there was no violent antipathy towards them. They were either acknowledged or ignored.

One saving grace for Gerry, as far as the 'chaps' were concerned, was that he had bombed the Old Bailey. That symbolic strike, at what was, for us, a hated symbol of oppression, endeared him to quite a few. The further knowledge that he had come within a whisker of blowing up New Scotland Yard, too, added to his popularity. Quite a few of us had contemplated doing just that at one time or another.

On a personal level I found him to be pleasant, intelligent, shy and extremely naive about crime. Before the actual bombing, he had never committed a criminal act in his life, not even a minor one. Ironically, he was strongly against conventional criminal activity *per se*.

This latter fact was only revealed to me during one of our infrequent 'escape committee' meetings. We had been discussing what we were going to do after the escape. The IRA was relatively unorganized in England at this time. Ian and I were to provide the getaway vehicle and the safe house. Gerry had promised us help to get away overseas.

This meant that we would spend several days in the safe house before leaving. As neither Ian nor I had any money, we had been discussing a bit of work he had been looking at before his arrest. It was a large, general Post Office in North London. A determined team could take upwards of a hundred grand. This would come in very handy for our future lives on the run.

I asked Gerry and Malcolm if they would like to join us in the venture. There was a stony, embarrassed silence. It transpired that neither had stolen anything in their whole lives before; both were ideologically opposed to stealing and, lastly, in Gerry's case, the IRA wouldn't approve.

I was astounded. Here were two men who would think nothing of blowing up public buildings, yet they baulked at armed robbery.

'Malcolm, think of it as redistributing wealth in an oppressive capitalist society,' I said with just a trace of irony. Embarrassed, he shook his head and refused to be moved.

'Gerry, you can give your share to the IRA.'

Equally embarrassed he mumbled, 'I'm a bomber, Norman, not a robber. There's others do the robbing.'

The logic of this Republican division of labour largely escaped me. I was on the verge of asking if there was anything in their respective party manifestos that prohibited escaping and possibly bashing a screw on the way out, but I refrained. Ian had reassured me that both were keen to take part.

Now there were four of us awaiting the removal of the scaffolding. At long last the renovation finished and the contractors started to dismantle it. However, we suddenly had another problem. Three Libyan terrorists had been arrested, and they were lodged in 'A'-wing Seg. As a direct result, security at the jail was increased. Unmarked cars full of armed police encircled the jail day and night. We wouldn't be able to make a move until the Libyans were transferred.

More months passed and the Libyans were finally deported. The jail was returned to normal. We readied ourselves to make our move.

At first it was just a wild rumour. Soon the whole nick was buzzing with the story. A young fella had been killed in the Seg.

I found it hard to believe at first. 'A'-wing Seg. was quite civilized as punishment blocks go. There were no systematic, regular beatings. However, Steven Smith had definitely died in a punishment cell in the Seg.

The trouble had started on 'C' wing. Steven, barely in his 20s, was doing four years. He was backward rather than mentally retarded. With his nerdy looks and National Health glasses, he was more inadequate than criminal. He was awkward and argumentative and regularly fell foul of the screws.

He had been taken to the Seg. after his umpteenth argument with a screw. The official version was that he had died sometime during the night. They said he had been found hanging from his window bars. There were several discrepancies though. Further rumours were coming from Seg. that he had been beaten up.

Whatever the real facts, the authorities didn't help themselves with their subsequent secretive behaviour. With feeling running high, they didn't want to carry the body out through 'A' wing, past cells full of prisoners. So they put Steven in a sack and carried him down the narrow, circular staircase at the rear of the Seg. Once in the yard, they put the sack in the back of an unmarked van and drove out of the prison.

The whole episode lacked a certain dignity. It smacked of a cover-up. Several lifers remarked that it was similar to details in their own cases. A further surprise came when it was revealed that the body was quickly cremated and, it was rumoured, without the permission of the family.

The jail was now in complete uproar. Men who had been quietly doing their time were vociferous in their protests. There was a move for something to be done. A sit-down protest was mooted.

The inquest was quickly convened. When the story was reported in the press the headline in the local paper read, DID WARDERS MURDER THIS MAN? Conflicting evidence was presented. One prisoner from the Seg. said that he had heard a scuffle, then silence. Another said that Steven had asked him for a cigarette during the night, yet his family and friends swore he had never smoked in his life.

A rope was presented, made from torn pieces of canvas sheet. When asked to tear a strip off the same sheet, the 19-stone exhibits officer was not able to do so. Yet Steven was frail and had a partially crippled hand. There was more in a similar vein, all quite suspicious.

However, the Prison Service closed ranks as usual. In the final analysis it came down to the word of a prisoner against that of a prison officer. The jury returned an 'open' verdict. It wasn't what the authorities wanted, but it was all they were going to get. As far as they were concerned, the matter was closed.

Back in 'D' wing it was far from closed. We hadn't expected anything from the inquest. It was all part and parcel of the system. And the system always worked to protect itself. The only justice we would get was that which we made ourselves. We decided on a sit-down.

Within the circle of our 'escape committee' we were astounded at how accelerating events had overtaken us. We were intent on escaping, that would be our personal statement against the system. Suddenly, though, there was a major matter of principle at stake. We had to take part. Enthusiastically, we joined in organizing the protest.

The following day over 200 men sat down in 'D' wing. There were scattered protests on other wings. The prison ground to a halt, and several wing Governors came to negotiate. It was a significant incident.

As much as I felt my violent nature to be indefensible, at heart I considered myself to be a reasonable, even honourable man. Surely, even the Home Office could see the rightness of a protest about a murder, albeit one committed by screws. I didn't expect a commendation for my part in the protest, but I didn't expect outright condemnation either.

Two days later, early on a Saturday morning, I was shanghaied. Ten screws came to my cell, I was taken to reception, loaded into a van and sent on my way to Parkhurst. The following day Malcolm was shanghaied to Gartree. In disposing of two of the ringleaders of the sit-down, they had unwittingly disposed of two would-be escapers.

There were still two left, though, and Ian and Gerry were determined to carry on. Ian knew the whole plan and where the various materials were to be obtained. The escape was scheduled for the following Saturday.

During the week Ian put aside two sets of screws' overalls and two shirts. He had checked them for size, and they were a good fit. He retrieved the two badges. Back in his cell he set about making the two caps to go with them. As he left the laundry late on Friday afternoon he carried the overalls and shirts with him.

Saturday dawned, with Ian and Gerry readying themselves for a visit. Later, as Gerry sat with his wife, Ian discussed last-minute details with a cousin. He told him where the car was to be left and at what time. As he got up from the visit, he took the key from his cousin and hid it in his mouth. The rub-down search proved to be no problem.

The afternoon seemed to drag on interminably. Both stayed out of the way in Ian's cell lest some fluke attract attention to them. When tea was finally served, neither could face it.

With tea over, the wing settled down to an evening's association. Some went to their cells and banged up; others sat playing cards and talking; the remainder played games or watched TV. At the far end of 'D' wing, beyond table 13, a hundred men sat impassively in front of the big TV set.

Inside Ian's cell on the 'ones', he and Gerry put on their disguise. They paused momentarily as a friend stopped by to give them the hammer he had borrowed from the wing office. Then, with a few quick adjustments to the hats, they were ready.

Ostensibly, the fellas on table 13 were sitting quietly, playing cards. In reality, they were scanning the wing, watching the movements of the screws. Suddenly, the nearest screw was down by the centre and out of clear view of the end gate. The signal was given.

As nonchalantly as they could manage, Ian and Gerry strolled from the cell. They passed table 13, circled the body of men watching TV and approached the gate. Without looking back, Ian opened the gate with the key, walked through with Gerry, then locked it again.

Their passing hadn't gone unnoticed though. A couple of the TV watchers had stood up and were sheepishly making their way back towards the main body of the wing. All of the complement of table 13 now stood up and glared at them. 'Sit down,' they mouthed. The offenders returned to their seats.

After the warmth of the wing, the cold, evening air felt stimulating. Staying close to the end of the building, Ian and Gerry headed into the enfolding darkness, across the small yard to the laundry gate.

With one quick movement Ian knocked the padlock from its hasp. He had acquired the knack robbing wagons as a child in the goods yard near his North London home. Using the key again, he let them both into the laundry, locking the gate behind them. He rested the broken padlock back in its hasp. It would pass a cursory inspection.

Together they broke into the Works' store, forced the tools cabinet open and got their first surprise. There were no bolt-croppers. Ian quickly ran to the partition. The plasterboard disintegrated with his frantic attack, revealing the second surprise. A reinforcement of thick steel mesh stood between them and the paint shop. With only the tools they had, they wouldn't be able to get the ladders.

Gerry looked deflated.

'Think, think,' cried Ian, screwing up his face and clenching both fists. He glanced around the shop.

There, against a wall, stood a pair of steps. They were only eight-foot high though. Ian cut the retaining ropes and laid them flat on the floor. Now they were 16-foot long, but one of the eight-foot sections comprised just two lengths of wood.

Next, Ian turned to one of the massive tables that were used for folding sheets on. The strutting underneath was criss-crossed with wooden slats. He broke several of these free, then, with Gerry holding the whole construction steady, he nailed them across the steps as rungs. Finally, he fixed a length along each side of the steps to keep them open and rigid. Now he had a slightly rickety 16-foot ladder.

That should take care of the first fence. But he needed something for the wall. He scoured the shop again.

He tipped another of the massive tables on to its side, revealing long pieces of thick strutting. Cutting two eight-foot lengths free, he laid them side by side on the floor. Once again, he nailed wooden slats across them. He now had another makeshift ladder. They were ready for the move to the fence.

This next part would be largely a hit-and-miss affair. They didn't have a vantage-point from which to observe the comings and goings of the screws. They would just have to wait until a patrol went past, leave it a couple of minutes, then go and trust to luck.

They watched as the screw with the large, black German shepherd passed the end of 'C' wing. Silently, they followed their passage across 'C'-wing yard. They disappeared out of sight behind the blank end wall of the laundry, only to appear again crossing 'D'-wing yard. Finally, they went behind the end of 'D' wing and out of sight.

Ian counted up to 100, then opened the gate. Each carrying a ladder, they ran side by side to the nearest part of the fence. In the deathly quiet Ian threw the longest ladder up against the fence. In his mind he could imagine the turmoil that was soon to come: the lights, the sirens, the panic in the control-room. He started up the ladder.

The plan had been for him to go up first; the flimsy ladder wouldn't hold two. However, in the heat of the moment, Gerry climbed beside him. There was a grating sound as the foot of the ladder sunk into the gravel, then a sharp snap. Part of one leg had broken off, and the ladder slipped sideways.

With a strength born of desperation, Gerry threw the ladder he was carrying clear over the fence. Reaching upwards, he grasped the top of a panel and heaved himself up. He wobbled precariously on the top, swung over, then dropped to the ground.

For Ian, though, it was all over. Gerry stood a good five inches taller than him. When the ladder broke and slipped sideways it sounded Ian's death knell. Stretch as he might, he just couldn't reach the top of the fence now.

'Go on, go on,' he cried at Gerry, pausing on the other side of the fence. Immediately galvanized, Gerry grabbed the short ladder and made for the corner where the walls met.

Sirens were blaring now; there was the sound of running feet; cons were shouting encouragement from the wing. Gerry was oblivious to it all. Carefully, he placed the ladder against the wall. Gingerly, he climbed upwards. Relief flooded through him as his fingers clasped the thick, black camera cable. It was all behind him now as he hoisted himself up to sit astride the wall.

'Stay right where you fucking are.'

The voice seemed to come out of nowhere. Startled, he gazed around, blinking in the harsh glare of the outside floodlights.

'Sit still.' The voice came again.

There, below him on the road that ran alongside the prison, stood a man wearing a dark suit. Next to him stood another, similarly attired. Both were facing him, legs apart, arms outstretched towards him. As Gerry focused more clearly, he saw the guns they were holding in their hands.

He looked back inside the jail in time to see several screws surround Ian. He watched as they led him away. He turned again, as he heard a noise outside, further up the road. A van with a flashing blue light sped towards the two men on the ground.

With a deep sigh, Gerry threw back his head and stared at the heavens. So much space, so much distance. He mused that this was probably as close as he would get to freedom for a very long time. With a shrug of resignation, he hoped it would be enough to sustain him through the long months of solitary that were to come.

Ever the warrior, Ian continued to rebel throughout his sentence. Tear-up followed tear-up, escape attempt followed escape attempt, he was moved from jail to jail. Finally, the flesh failed the spirit. In his 16th year Ian suffered a severe mental breakdown. For a long while his sanity hung in the balance. It was four more years before he was finally released, damaged in mind and body.

Of late, he is much better. Occasionally, his great spirit still shines through. He lives in reduced circumstances in his beloved North London. I see him regularly. He is still one of my closest friends.

Not long after the Scrubs escape, Gerry Kelley was transferred to Northern Ireland. He escaped from the Maze in a mass break-out. He was recaptured in Holland, only to be freed again. He is now a member of Sinn Fein's executive committee. He has recently been seen at the side of Gerry Adams at public engagements.